Thinker Task Cards
Independent Activities to Stimulate Creative Thinking

by
Lisa Rogulic-Newsome

illustrated by Corbin Hillam

Cover by Corbin Hillam

Copyright © 1992, Good Apple

ISBN No. 0-86653-681-7

Printing No. 987654321

Good Apple
1204 Buchanan St., Box 299
Carthage, IL 62321-0299

SIMON & SCHUSTER *A Paramount Communications Company*

Dedication

I'd like to dedicate this book to two people who have been of paramount importance in my life: first, my very, very special grandmother, Bernice E. Horrall, who started early on stressing to me how very creative and bright I was...and finally I believed it!

Second, I'd like to dedicate this book to Lester Plotner, my second superintendent, whose never-ending faith in my ability has caused me to aspire to great heights, both professionally and in my writing career. You never gave up on me, and I never gave up on myself. Thank you so much, Mr. Plotner, for superintendents like you are few and far between. You are a beautiful person.

Also, my never-ending thanks goes to my mother, Louise Rogulic, and to my husband, John Newsome, for all their hard work on making this book a success. Thank you both from the bottom of my heart.

Table of Contents

GA1415

iv

GA1415

v

GA1415

About This Book

Thinker Task Cards
34 tasks per grade level
Full range of difficulty, grades 3-8
Written on "two per page" sheets–able to be laminated

Focusing on Bloom's Six Levels of Higher Order Thinking

- Knowledge–the ability to know
- Comprehension–the ability to understand
- Application–the ability to apply knowledge to new situations
- Analysis–the ability to break down into parts
- Synthesis–the ability to create, design, invent
- Evaluation–the ability to judge

Pinpointing Different Levels of Creativity

- Fluency–generating a frequency of responses
- Flexibility–able to shift one's thinking from one area to another
- Originality–creating one truly unique and different idea
- Elaboration–adding details to creations and works

Incorporating a Variety of Subjects

- Mathematics
- English
- Social Studies
- Science
- Problem Solving

Multitopical Tasks

- Filling empty moments with challenges
- Holding students accountable

A Multitude of Ways to Beat the Boredom Blues!

GA1415

Introduction

How Can You Use This Book?

(Let me count the ways...)

1. Supplemental Enrichment Tasks
   a. Great teachers often present a lesson with loads of practice only to discover three to five of their best students have completed the practice with extra time left and with nothing to do. The "Task Cards Under Wraps" (TCUW) will offer high level thinking activities which are both stimulating and creative in nature.

   b. Students who complete their assigned work and choose a TCUW could continue to elaborate on it long after the period has ended. All they would need is a special large envelope marked "Task Cards Under Wraps" continuously kept in their desks to hold their TCUW projects.

2. Center Ideas
   a. Successful teachers can draw upon their imaginations and creative juices while designing an intriguing Top Secret center which focuses in on the TCUW. An example might be a large box with the words "Task Cards Under Wraps" on the top, covered with dark-colored gift wrap, and consisting of a large hand-sized hole for students to reach in for TCUW's. Another example might be a gift wrap covered box with curtain hooks across the side on which they can hang the TCUW's.

   b. TCUW's can either be written on long pieces of paper and placed inside envelopes or written on the envelopes themselves which are then folded to display the words "Task Cards Under Wraps."

   c. Talented teachers can pick and choose TCUW's with either topics matching student interests or a specific grade level(s) matching their own population of children.

3. Lesson Plans
   a. Innovative teachers can choose one envelope ahead of time and use the "Task Cards Under Wraps" as an anticipatory set as well as a lesson or activity.

   b. A TCUW can be chosen by a teacher on the spur of the moment to fill an empty time interval on which he/she hadn't counted.

   c. Resourceful teachers can assign certain TCUW's to substitutes to use as lesson fillers while the teacher is absent.

   d. The TCUW's can also be used as starting points for research projects or creative lessons, upon which the inspired teacher can elaborate using some of his/her very own ideas!

4. Independent Study Projects
   a. In a gift or special resource room, the TCUW's could be used as special Independent Study Projects which might be primarily done outside the classroom and then eventually shared with the class.

   b. In a regular classroom, the TCUW's could also be used for Independent Study Projects to be completed partially at home and partially at school. In this way, the conscientious teacher would be able to keep tabs on how his/her students were progressing with their projects, while also focusing the main responsibility for work on the students themselves.

5. Incentive Reward Program:
   a. As a special incentive or reward for finishing their work early, students would be "allowed" to choose a special TCUW to work on for the remainder of the period, or for extra credit at some later time.

   b. Students could "earn" time to work on TCUW's which would develop self-esteem and raise self-confidence in their everyday work. It would also allow for more time-on-task because students would desire to go to the Top Secret center and would use their class time more wisely.

6. A Grab Bag of Tasks
   Even super teachers find themselves in a rut now and then, teaching the 3R's. Break out of this mold by filling a large bag with selected TCUW's similar in the length of time it takes to accomplish each. Then on a rainy Friday afternoon or any other appropriate time, go around the room and allow students to "grab" a task and complete it within the allotted amount of time.

7. Simple Shoe Box Approach
   Separate the tasks into the various discipline areas (for example, science, math, social studies and English). Place each stack into a different shoe box and when the bright English student finishes early, direct him/her to the shoe box marked *English* and ask him/her to take out a task and complete it. Or when the social studies assignment is done early by an intellectually accelerated student, simply steer him to the Social Studies shoe box, ask him to choose a TCUW, and watch him fill up his remaining time with intrigue and adventure.

GA1415

DO YOU WANT THIS IN YOUR CLASSROOM...
BATTLES
OBSTRUCTION
REPETITION
EXASPERATION
DULLNESS
OBSTINACY
MONOTONY
BOREDOM?

OR WOULD YOU CHOOSE...
EXHILERATING
e**XP**ERIENCES
CAPTIVATING
INTERESTING
TERRIFIC
EXPLOSIVE
MASTERFUL
ENTERTAINING
NECESSARY
TEACHING?
EXCITEMENT?

CHOOSE THE ACTIVITIES IN THIS BOOK!

X

GA1415

HOME CALLS

Receiving a phone call from someone you don't know can be a big responsibility. If you answer in the wrong way, something awful might happen. If an individual is calling for someone in your family, and that family member is not home, what kinds of information do you need from the caller? And what kinds of information should you *give* the caller?

(003, Social Studies, Comprehension)

I DON'T LIKE THAT!

You are being teased by your friends. It annoys you in the worse way, but up until now, you've kept your mouth shut. Well, now's your chance! What are at least five ways to approach this problem without anyone getting hurt? Make a list.

(003, Social Studies, Analysis, Fluency)

GA1415

CURDS AND WHEY

Little Miss Muffet,

Sat on a tuffet,

Eating her curds and whey. (What are they?)

Along came a spider,

Who sat down beside her,

And frightened Miss Muffet away.

First, try to discover what curds and whey are in a dictionary or encyclopedia. Second, name each single kind of spider that could have come down beside Miss Muffet. Make a list.

(003, English, Comprehension, Fluency)

ENORMOUS SUPERSAURUS

The dinosaurs called the Sauropods were the heaviest and biggest land animals that ever lived. The giant supersaurus was over thirty feet (9.1 m) tall and it weighed up to 100,000 pounds (4.5 t). That is as much as forty compact cars!

What kinds of foods do you think the supersaurus ate and how much per day? Make up a daily menu. (He probably didn't eat scrambled eggs and ham for breadkfast either!)

(003, Science, Synthesis)

GA14

SWEETS FOR THE SWEET

They say you are only what you eat,

And that one thing to avoid is the sweet.

Well, Sally avoided nothing on her binge,

And what she ate would make anyone cringe.

She gobbled 30 eclairs quick right down,

And when she got done she looked just like a clown.

She went on to gorge 50 chocolate malts,

But never recognized any of her faults.

Finally, she shoved down 90 chocolate bars,

And she became one of food's biggest stars!

How much food and drink did Sally devour,

Before her taste buds went sad and sour?

(003, Mathematics, Problem Solving, Addition)

DUMB AS A DODO

You've all heard of the term "dumb as a dodo." Well, it was discovered around the 1500's on the island of Mauritius. The term "dumb as a dodo" came about as these dodo birds were so easy to catch but not because they were any dumber.

Many famous sayings came about because of things having to do with nature.

Imagine a society where all the inhabitants come from popular sayings: slippery as an eel, wise as an owl, tall as a giraffe, graceful as a gazelle, pretty as a peacock, etc.

Design this society, making sure to include the pecking order (highest in the society down to the lowest), laws, money, religion(s), jobs, government, entertainment, garbage disposal, etc.

(003, Social Studies, Synthesis)

GA1415

PANDAMONIUM

Giant pandas are very large animals, as you might think when you hear their name. They are almost five feet (1.52 m) long when fully grown and can weigh over 200 pounds (90 kg). But giant pandas aren't really giants in the same way that an elephant is a giant. One average elephant weighs more than thirty giant pandas.

If you had ninety giant pandas, how many elephants would their weight equal?

(003, Mathematics, Problem Solving, Division)

TWO FAMOUS BILLS

Wild Bill Hickok and Buffalo Bill Cody were two legendary characters from the Wild, Wild West. They starred in shows which featured such things as horseback riders, covered wagons, animal tamers, acrobats and other acts which drew large crowds.

Research Wild Bill and Buffalo Bill. Try to discover what made these two men so famous during a time in history when becoming well-known was a hard thing to do.

(003, Social Studies, Analysis)

4

GA1415

IT'S ALL ROCK AND ROLL TO ME!

Betty had four rock and roll albums,
While Jessica had six albums of punk rock.
Steve liked his nine albums of rhythm and blues,
And then all of them had a real shock!

Elyse had twenty jazz albums.
In addition, Arnold loved his sixteen musical quartets.
Joe adored his fifteen country and westerns,
And most of all, Andrea took all bets!

She had the best singing voice,
And could outsolo anyone in her place.
Her only accompaniment was the piano
And Willie and his enormous lead bass.

Now you, as a mathematical performer,
Can even beat Andrea out,
Just count up the albums' total,
And then strike up your vocal chords and shout!

(003, Mathematics, Problem Solving, Addition)

STRETCH!

Giraffes have extremely long necks which enable them to eat the greenery off of low-lying trees. Their long necks also enable them to reach across obstacles to watering holes.

Name as many other animals as possible who have long necks in relation to their bodies. Then write a poem about the trials and tribulations of having a long neck.

(003, Science, Synthesis)

GA1415

FLIGHTLESS BIRDS

Ostriches, rheas and emus will eat almost anything shiny. Some people even believe that these flightless birds can digest metal, but that is not true. The metal remains in their gizzards.

Imagine a list of all the shiny metal things which birds might eat. Then think of five more things and add to each one that you've brainstormed. Then add them all up and see how many you've collected, just as the birds do.

(003, Mathematics, Problem Solving, Addition)

CALLING ALL PHONE BOOKS

In an average city, there are approximately 100,000 names in the city's telephone directory. Is your number listed? Everyone receives a new phone book once a year. Phone books can be used for pressing flowers, as a paperweight, etc.

Thousands of people use the phone book for many different purposes. Make a list of at least ten reasons why someone might want to use the phone directory.

(003, Social Studies, Fluency, Application)

GA1415

ORANGES ARE NOT JUST FOR EATING

An orange is a reddish-yellow, round, edible, citrus fruit, with a sweet juicy pulp, usually used for juicing or in the case of a navel orange, used for eating. Orange is also a color consisting of reddish-yellow or yellowish-red.

Invent a new holiday which centers its theme and decorations around the color of orange.

Or design an all-orange greeting card.

Or write an apology to Oscar, the orange orangutan, for something terrible or secret that you once did.

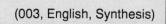

(003, English, Synthesis)

A THANKSGIVING CONVERSATION

Ever imagine what it might have been like to have been at Plymouth Rock? Imagine what it might have been like sitting down to dinner with the Pilgrims and the Indians. In honor of Thanksgiving, write a conversation which might have occurred between a Pilgrim and an Indian.

(003, Social Studies, Synthesis)

GA1415

AN ARTISTIC HISTORICAL MOMENT

Are you good in art? Do you like to draw? Well, here's your chance! Think about something in history and then paint or draw a mural of an important historical moment or event. Use as many details as possible in your finished product. Be as vivid with your final product as possible.

(003, Social Studies, Elaboration, Synthesis)

IT'S RAINING CATS AND DOGS

"A dog is man's best friend." "Cats have nine lives." Owls answer the question, "Who? Who?" There have been many quotations written about people's pets as well as other animals too!

"It's raining cats and dogs!" Where do you think this saying came from? Draw a picture which shows its "actual" meaning!

(003, English, Application)

GA1415

EYE SPY

There once was a ferocious monster,
Who lived in the woods so green.
And he had the biggest bunch of eyes,
That you have ever quite seen!

One eye was just for spying on others.
Another pair of eyes watched during the night.
A trio of eyes saw the food it would devour,
And twenty mini eyes were just for sight!

A long extended eye swept the ground for bees,
While a short one stared straight into the prey's eyes.
Fourteen purple eyes would wink and smile,
While five other eyes had their peepers full of cries.

Well, your job as the monster's friend so true,
Is to figure out the exact number of eyes so new…
The monster had to fend against others that might try to
Commit crimes against this friend, oh so blue.

(How many eyes did the ferocious monster have?)

(003, Mathematics, Problem Solving, Addition)

MONEY ISN'T FUNNY

Pretend that the American money exchange is not working and therefore will have to be changed. In other words, there is no more money as we know it!

Design your own monetary (money) system, including both currency (coins) and cash (bills). What will each of your coins and bills stand for? Explain your monetary system in detail.

(003, Social Studies, Synthesis)

GA1415

THIS RATTLE DOESN'T COME FROM A BABY!

A rattlesnake gets its name by a rattle on its tail. It is used to warn animals and people to stay away. The sound of the rattle can be very loud, and the noise can carry for long distances up to sixty feet (18.2 m).

If there were ten rattlers on a hill, and each one was rattling as loud as it could, how many total feet (meters) could the sound travel?

(003, Mathematics, Problem Solving, Multiplication)

A HAIRLESS WONDER!

People have hair. Dolls have hair. Wigs are made of real hair–sometimes. However, some animals do not have hair. Lizards, snakes, turtles, and penguins are all animals without hair or fur. Bunny rabbits have fur. Polar bears have fur. Lions have fur.

List at least twenty other animals with fur.

(003, Science, Fluency)

GA1415

DOGS AND THEIR WALKS

Little Bobby got a new puppy,
For a birthday present one year.
The puppy licked and barked and cried,
And everyone commented, "What a dear!"
The puppy, Al, left behind three brothers in a cage,
They were sad to see him go—actually, what an outrage!
His two sisters were farmed out to different families,
But no matter where his family went, they always loved the trees.
If each of Al's brothers and sisters
Took two walks every single day...
And went up to five trees during each walk,
How many total trees do you say?

(In other words, how many total trees did they walk up to?)

(003, Math, Problem Solving, Addition, Multiplication)

A ROCKY RELATIONSHIP

Azurite, malochite, and wulfinite are considered to be precious minerals and can be found in several different areas in the United States. Quartz, onyx, and sapphire are some other rocks and gems found in rock collections. Many young rock collectors have some form of these minerals in their rock collections.

Imagine that a new type of mineral has just been found and YOU are the discoverer!

Write about your feelings and fears as you decide how to share your findings with the rest of the world.

(003, Science, Analysis)

THEY'RE NOT ALL NUTS!

Although elephants may eat an occasional peanut here and there, they also eat 100,000 pounds (45,000 kg) of hay, 12,000 pounds (5400 kg) of alfalfa, 1500 gallons (5670 l) of mixed grains, 2000 potatoes, 3000 cabbages, apples, carrots, and other vegetables per year as well. Elephants could be considered mammoth eaters.

Create a telegram from a jumbo elephant to his favorite "nut."

(003, Science, Synthesis)

I SCREAM FOR ICE CREAM!

Mmm, mmm, good! Mmm, mmm, good! That's what ice cream is, mmm, mmm, good!

Write the directions for how to construct a Rainbow Parfait, a Banana Snowball Split, an Earthquake Freeze, a Triple-Thick Pineapple Fluff, and a Never-on-Sundae.

Make sure to make your recipes in the shapes of their food dishes. (For example, the recipe for a sundae might be made inside a drawn sundae bowl.)

(003, English, Synthesis)

GA141

IF YOU WERE...

If you were a baboon, would you beat your tummy?

If you were an ice-cream sundae, would you be yummy?

If you were a Bobbsey Twin, would you solve crimes?

If you were a gumball machine, would you collect dimes?

If you were a straight-A student, would you work hard?

If you were a cow, would you make lard?

If you had ten wishes, what oh what would you be?

Just write them down, go to town, and see Mickey Mouse III.

(Just kidding about the last one!)

(003, English, Comprehension, Problem Solving)

CIRCUS FEVER

It was a circus to end all circuses,

The fifteen clowns were fit as it would seem.

Forty acrobats flew across the Big Top,

And the man in a cannon was a scream.

The fat lady and the skinny man were paired up,

While the small boy held in his hands an enormous snake.

Six tightwalkers made sure they were dainty,

While all the unicyclist did was shake and bake.

How many circus performers,

Performed under the Big Top that day...

In front of thousands of roaring little youngsters,

Who had arrived just to see them all play?

(003, Mathematics, Problem Solving, Addition)

GA1415

THE FISHING FLU

Four boys went fishing in a canoe.

To see how many fish they could boo.

As the day grew long but really just flew,

There were a few secrets only the boys knew.

It took cheese, a hook, and a pickle too,

In order to do what they wanted to do.

There was a cow on the bank "moo moo."

And a flock of geese just tried to woo woo.

The question of the day, is this, you see,

If there were 18 geese who wanted to flee,

And 14 cows on bended knee,

With 142 fish beneath the sea…

How many animals were close nearby

The boys in their canoe who were willing to try?

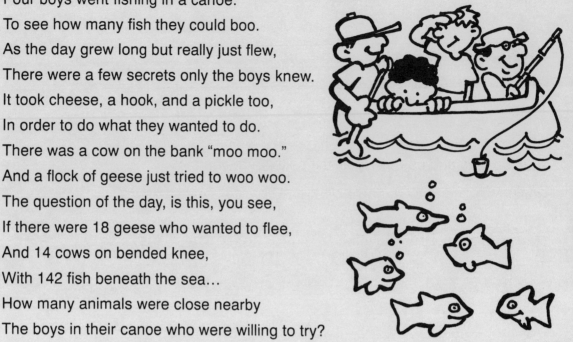

(003, Mathematics, Problem Solving, Addition)

MONSTER MASH

Many television and comic strip monsters have been created over the past 100 years. Godzilla, The Abominable Snowman, Wolfman, Dracula and Frankenstein are just a few.

King Kong has come to town, crunching buildings as he goes. As the city mayor, it is your job to stop him! What's your plan of action going to be? Give a step-by-step plan that you will use.

(003, Social Studies, Problem Solving)

GA1415

MODGE PODGE

9 bricks of gold, a green Jell-O mold, and a TV oh so clear,

6 pots of stew, a clock so new, and an empty can of root beer.

18 walks, 97 talks and a crowded room so dim,

42 men, a cat who counts to 10 and Jack that's what we call him.

4 patio chairs, 16 orchestra stairs and a bright crayon that's true blue,

2 rocket ships, a dog that does flips and 7 hats that are so new.

Your job is to add up quickly all things that are seen,

On the TV by a boy named Paul, who was all the while so keen.

(003, Mathematics, Problem Solving, Addition)

SEACHING FOR A CINQUAIN

Have you ever heard of a cinquain? Cinquains are unrhymed poems with five lines. For example:

Spider (2-syllable topic)

Furry walker (4 syllables describing topic)

Stalking, searching, killing (6 syllables expressing action)

So beautifully constructed (8 syllables expressing feeling)

Monster (2-syllable synonym for topic)

Write two cinquains, one about bicycles and one about pandas.

Bicycles	Perfect Pandas
1.	1.
2.	2.
3.	3.
4.	4.
5.	5.

(003, English, Synthesis)

GA1415

PURPLE PEOPLE EATERS

Purple is a dark color that is a blend of red and blue, as well as being elaborate in your writing (003, purple prose). The Purple Heart is awarded to members of the armed forces for being wounded in action against the enemy. A purple martin is a North American swallow with bluish-black plumage or feathers. A purple-fringed orchid is one of two North American orchids with purple-fringed flowers.

Make up a funny phrase about purple things. Or design a home remedy for the dreaded disease "Purpleitis." Or create a purple mobile made up only of purple things. Or write and give a sales pitch to the class, concerning a creative purple outfit that will explode into the fashion world!

(003, English, Synthesis)

IT'S ALL IN A NAME

In the world of pre-teens and teenagers comes the age of wimps, bullies, geeks, dweebs, royal "pains," prunes, punks, radicals, brains, dudes, and other assorted labels. All of these labels represent a different kind of class of student or non-student. Labels can hurt people or they can just name.

Your job is to develop your very own hierarchy of children your age with new names and definitions. Be complete in your description of each.

(003, Social Studies, Synthesis)

GA14

FLAGS MEAN FREEDOM

Flags are used for many different things. Some countries use their national flags as symbols of freedom and others as a pledge of allegiance to the government. Every country has a totally unique flag, unlike that of any other country.

Your job is to create a flag booklet, where you draw and color the flags of ten countries in the world and write the name of the country in the lower right-hand corner of each page. In addition, include at least two facts which might highlight sports, foods, government, holidays, type of people, products imported and exported, religions, etc.

(003, Social Studies, Application)

TALL TALES TWIST TIME

Tall tales tell outlandish stories where everything is a real exaggeration! In a tall tale, people are 30 feet (9 m) tall, animals eat 500 pounds (225 kg) of food a day, and aliens live next door. Tall tales are basically lies told in jest!

Write a tall tale about an aardvark who grew to be 40 feet tall (12 m) and weighed 1000 pounds (450 kg).

(003, English, Synthesis)

A NAME IS A NAME IS A NAME

Our names are very important to us as they symbolize just exactly who we are and may also tell a little about what we are like. For example, someone named Buddy might be a good friend to all who know him.

Illustrate your first name while feeling the following emotions: anger, sadness, happiness, surprise, and fright. Now try the same five with your last name. How do they compare? In other words, write your name while pretending to feel anger, sadness, happiness, surprise, and fright. Figure out how they relate to one another.

(003, Social Studies, Comprehension)

A PLANT'S DEFENSE SYSTEM

If, in the days of the dinosaur, the animals had eaten all of the plants, then they would have all died out. However, the plants did several things to defend themselves: developed slippery coatings, spines, and grew better, etc.

If there were two hundred plants and each one grew three different defense mechanisms, how many total ways of defending themselves would that amount to?

(003, Math, Problem Solving, Multiplication)

GA14

STORY TIME

Every day, you're asked to read a story in your class. After reading that story for your class or on your own, illustrate a poster about a specific scene or character in the book or story, using at least three different mediums (felt, sequins, paint, pipe cleaners, clay, etc.).

(004, English, Comprehension)

MAP SKILLS

Everyone has a hometown, one where he was born or grew up.

On the map, if you pinpoint your hometown and then draw an imaginary circle encompassing a 300-mile (483 km) radius, make a list of all the cities you would find with populations over 100,000 persons.

(004, Social Studies, Application)

GA1415

TUT'S TOMB

In Egypt's earlier years, all the important people (kings, queens, etc.) were buried in tombs after death. Egyptians believed there was to be a later life, one that they would come back into during some later time. Because they believed this, they were often buried with their riches and their belongings. The bodies became mummified which was a special way to preserve the body over hundreds of years.

Research King Tut's tomb and all that was found in it. (His real name was Tutankhamon.) The tomb has been on display all over the world during the past several years. See if you can discover where the remains are now.

(004, Social Studies, Knowledge)

A TURTLE WITHOUT A SHELL MEANS NOTHING

Turtles are unique critters. They carry their houses on their backs in the form of a large shell, totally unlike any other animal. Like dinosaurs, turtles are primitive reptiles that first appeared on Earth about two million years ago. Turtles haven't changed much over the years and their shells give them excellent protection, for they can just disappear inside if approached by an enemy. Turtles fit into these three groups: fresh-water turtles, sea turtles, and tortoises.

Find out all that you can about these three categories of turtles in some different reference books. Create a mobile complete with pictures of the three turtle types.

Write a brief description under each picture.

(004, Science, Application)

GA1415

WIGGLELINEDOODLES!

A pattern is defined as a "form or model used for imitation."

Make a pattern with a crayon. Take another crayon and continue the pattern for a second or two and then change the pattern. Continue along the path until you have used all the colors available to you. Now guess what? You have just created a Wigglelinedoodle!

Now write a funny Wigglelinedoodle poem about your picture.

(004, English, Synthesis)

PICK A PROBLEM

Sculptures can be made of papier-mâché, clay, or just about any material(s) which you have on hand. There are very famous sculptures like Picasso's right on down to those made by you and your classmates.

Your task is to create a sculpture made out of anything you wish to use, which focuses on one of the world's problems. Starvation, overpopulation, pollution, greenhouse effect, and endangered species are just a few.

(004, Social Studies, Synthesis)

GA1415

PROFESSIONAL WRESTLING

Big Joe weighed in at 178 pounds,

While Eddie, the Funswick Manson,

Had 298 pounds in his mounds.

Marvin, the Marvelous weighed in at 301,

While Sampson, the Super Duper with 310 had him won!

Danny the Greek had everyone beat with 325,

While 170-pound Daddy Mamma could hardly survive.

Stevie, the Supernatural, was the largest on the team,

With 427 under his belt, it looked like one big cream!

The question of the day and the one for you to solve,

What is the total weight of all the wrestlers,

And which wrestler reigned king and really will evolve?

(004, Mathematics, Problem Solving, Addition)

A SCORPION STING!

On North America alone, we have the Sonoran Desert, the Mojave Desert, and Death Valley, just to name a few deserts. Deserts contain sand, brush, sometimes cacti, and desert animals, and hold many different treasures.

Some of these deserts contain scorpions. Make a list of the procedures you should use if stung by a scorpion.

(004, Science, Application)

GA1415

UNBELIEVABLE ANIMAL ACTS!

We often associate a certain animal with a specific set of actions. For example, giraffes have long necks so they can strain to reach the leaves off of even the tallest trees. Anteaters have very long noses and tongues to scout after ants to eat. But what if animals we'd expect to act one way, all of a sudden did something totally unexpected? For instance, what if elephants could fly? Or what if zebras were champion tree-climbers? What if otters could roam the desert? Make up ten totally unbelievable animal acts and illustrate each one.

(004, Science, Synthesis)

SAVORING EVERY BITE!

Ice cream is one of America's most delectable taste treats. Ice cream is cold, sweet, tasty and creamy. People eat it while doing all sorts of things, like riding a bike, bantering on the phone, or going back and forth on the teeter-totter.

Write a description about the experience of eating an ice-cream cone *without* using any of these words: *delicious, cone, creamy, cold, lick, bite, tasty, tempting, appetizing* and *ice cream.*

(004, English Elaboration)

GA1415

MATHEMATICS MINGLE

Mathematics plays a different role in each of our lives, from bookkeeper to real estate genius. We use math to figure out how much money it will take to buy the things we want, to count the things we already have, and to imagine how much it will take to get the things we'll want in the future. Write and give a speech on the importance of math in our daily lives, especially your own.

(004, English, Mathematics, Synthesis)

BULLFIGHTING MEANS BRAVERY

Bullfighting may seem cruel and inhumane to many, but in Mexico it is a ceremony which shows bravery and death. Even the bulls which are used are raised especially for this purpose. A huge dilemma comes to many after seeing a bullfight, and now you are being asked to face the same dilemma. Is bullfighting right or wrong? Are we being fair to the bull to hit it with small knives, larger swords, and a huge sword in the end? How do you feel? Write about your feelings in a paper.

(004, Social Studies, English, Evaluation)

GA1415

GREEN IS KEEN

St. Patrick's Day brings about thoughts of leprechauns, green clovers, and a pot of gold.

For the green holiday, St. Patrick's Day, go through the green items you might find in a grocery store. Rank the products from the most expensive to the least expensive. Add the prices of all the products and determine one complete total.

(004, Mathematics, English, Analysis, Addition)

THE BALLOON FESTIVAL

At the balloon hunt one hot afternoon,

Balloon 4 went 80 miles quite soon.

Balloon 2 crept 42 miles really slow,

While Balloon 6 went 137 miles on the go, go, go!

Balloon 7 travelled only 1 thin mile,

Then sat down on the ground, and went out in style.

Balloon 1 was the fastest one of all,

It went 392 miles and didn't even fall.

Balloon 3 skated a smooth 43 miles,

Right into an accountant's income tax files!

Balloon 5 exploded after 291 miles were done,

And Balloon 8 flew 50 miles right into the sun.

Your problem on this hot, hot day,

Is to figure out how many miles were totally blown away!

(004, Mathematics, Problem Solving, Addition)

25

GA1415

POWERING A BICYCLE

A bicycle is defined as a "vehicle consisting of a tubular metal frame mounted on two large wire-spoked wheels, one behind the other, and equipped with handlebars and a saddle-like seat; it is propelled by foot pedals or sometimes by a small gasoline motor."

First, make a list and name all the other vehicles you can think of with wheels. Second, name all the other ways you can think of, real or imaginary, that could power a bicycle by means other than by manpower or by engine.

(004, Social Studies, Problem Solving, Fluency)

RED REVEALS ITSELF

Red is the color of tomatoes, chili peppers, apples, and hearts. Red is also one of the three primary colors at the lowest end of the visible color spectrum.

Design an announcement for the birth of a Red Devil, Red Hots, or Red Rover. Or write and give a persuasive speech to convince everyone that everything should be colored "RED." Or complete this story beginning: "I'm so mad at her, I'm seeing red!" Or use various shades of red crayons over different textures to create a "feelie" picture.

(004, English, Synthesis)

TWO HUMPS FOR CAMELS!

Did you know that llamas, alpacas, vicuna, and some other animals without humps are also called camels? Over the years, people have shipped camels to Australia and now there are over 50,000 of them living right there! If, for example, an equal number of camels were shipped to Australia over a ten-year period, how many were shipped each year?

(004, Mathematics, Problem Solving, Division)

NEWSPAPER ANTICS

Four cups, 7 pups, and 15 dresses dandy,

Six cats, 14 mats, and 20 wads of candy.

Eleven beans, 19 greens, and 40 niblets of rice,

62 pens, 17 Bens, and 15 Janets so nice.

27 noodles, 72 poodles, and a pretty angel so white,

One bowl of chili, 1 guy named Willie, and 1 airplane out of sight.

These were things that Gus read about in the newspaper one cloudy day,

Your job right now is to add them up and don't you dare delay!

(004, Mathematics, Problem Solving, Addition)

GA1415

GORILLA SONG

Gorillas yawn, huff, cough, and hiccup, just like people do. Gorillas are very much like people. They have many of the same movements and mannerisms as man. If you study a gorilla for a long enough period of time, you'll feel like you are staring back into a mirror!

Compose a song, made up of gorilla noises and gestures, that a gorilla might engage in.

(004, Science, Application)

SKATERS GALORE

At a skating rink one Sunday, a boy named Fred,

Was skating so quickly that he fell flat on his head!

He finally got up, but not until much later,

After 151 boys passed him and one lone skater.

Fred needed a rest so he leaned against the wall,

Another 247 skated by, very strong and very tall

Fifteen more clasped hands with a weakening Fred,

"How many skaters?" the ticker tape read.

You solve the problem with great haste and rapid speed!

A piece of paper and a pencil are two materials you may need.

(How many skaters total besides Fred?)

(004, Mathematics, Problem Solving, Addition)

GA14

DESERT REPTILES

Reptiles contain skin that can hold moisture inside their bodies and therefore make them free to live in drier places. They can also molt or shed their skins while growing into bigger bodies.

List ten desert reptiles, research them, and in a paper tell how they adapt to their climates.

(004, Science, Application)

FASHION ARTICLE

There are many different colors of outfits from which one could choose to wear to a party. The purpose of the party could have something to do with how you dress, too. If it was a Western party you might wear jeans, cowboy boots and a Western hat. If it was a masquerade party, you could wear any outfit and be in style.

Write a fashion article about a party you imagined where everyone wore green.

(004, English, Synthesis, Fluency)

GA1415

COUNTRY AWARENESS

An almanac shares with the reader many facts and figures he can't find anywhere else. Use the most recent World Almanac to answer the following questions:

1. Which is the newest country in the world?

2. Which is the oldest country in the world?

3. How many countries are there in the world?

4. What are the ten largest countries?

(004, Social Studies, Knowledge)

MARSUPIAL MAMAS

Baby opossums are usually born with many in the litter. They spend much of their first few months in their mother's pouch, like the other marsupials such as the kangaroo. After they are too large to ride in the pouch, they ride on mama's back, sometimes fourteen at a time. If there were ten opossums, each with fourteen babies on its back, how many total babies would that be?

(004, Mathematics, Problem Solving, Multiplication)

GA14

DESIGN A BUMPER STICKER!

Brainstorm the names of at least fifteen different vehicles—a car, a truck, a van. Then design a bumper sticker that could go on each one. For example: On a Chevrolet: "Ford really does have a better idea– buy a Chevrolet!"

FORD REALLY DOES HAVE A BETTER IDEA — BUY A CHEVROLET

(004, Social Studies, Application)

DANCING AND PRANCING

Now once in awhile everyone takes a chance,

And feels light enough on his feet to dance.

You can almost tell at a moment's glance,

If it's going to be a boing or will it be a prance?

Mary Ellen Dithers loved to dance, it's true,

She'd break dance, flashdance, and tango too.

In one long evening she danced so much,

That her dance card read 240 or such.

If Mary Ellen Dithers spent three minutes on each dance,

How many total minutes did she spend in a prance?

(004, Mathematics, Problem Solving, Multiplication)

BEE FACTS

The honeybee is small when contrasted to a human. But it can fly almost as fast as a human runs. It beats its wings an incredible 15,000 times every minute. Imagine that! Bees are truly remarkable creatures.

Research the bee family and make a list of at least fifteen facts that are of interest to you. Compile a "Bee Family of Facts" booklet, complete with diagrams.

(004, Science, Knowledge)

THE HEALTHY AT HEART

Many modern individuals are on health food kicks and really watch what they eat. These individuals believe that being healthy is the most important thing they can be. Each and every day, they eat only the healthiest of foods.

Survey at least five "Health Food Nuts" and determine what their diets are like. Then design the perfect week-long diet for the "Healthy at Heart."

(004, Social Studies, Analysis)

GA14

AN OSTRICH BY ANY OTHER NAME...

Rheas are flightless birds which roam the grasslands of South America. Some have even deemed them the "South American ostriches." You can find rheas and ostriches in many of the zoos in the United States.

Make a list of all the similarities and differences between rheas and ostriches. You may need to use an encyclopedia.

(004, Science, Analysis)

GRAMP'S RAMPAGE

There once lived an old man named Gramp,

Whom some might consider a tramp.

He caught 20 fish one Tuesday,

Around the San Francisco Bay,

And traded them all in for a $60 lamp.

On Wednesday Gramp found a really nice camp,

And in the garbage can there was a very valuable stamp.

The stamp was worth $363 or so they say,

So Gramp traded it in for cash and yelled, "Hurray!"

He bought 33 umbrellas off a ramp,

How much did each umbrella cost Gramp?

(004, Mathematics, Problem Solving, Division)

 GA1415

BEE ROLES

In a bee colony, there are many different jobs that the different kinds of bees hold. Just as in society, each person has his own job to hold. To demonstrate that you understand the roles of the queen, drone, and worker bees, write and put on a skit displaying their positions in the hive.

(004, Science, Synthesis)

NO LIE'N

Powerful muscles in a lion's chest and in his legs give the lion an unbelievable amount of strength. Therefore, a lion can knock down animals three times bigger than it is. Given the following lions' weights, figure out how large the creatures might be that each lion could hold down:

a. 353; b. 162; c. 478; d 342; e. 290; f. 184

(004, Mathematics, Problem Solving, Multiplication)

GA141

THE PIG LATIN CODE

Pig Latin is a kind of coded language that children and adults like to use to disguise what they're saying. In order to speak Pig Latin, take the first consonant blend or letter from the start of a word, place it at the end of the word, and add the sound of *ay* to it. To those words beginning with a vowel, don't change the word but rather add *way* to the end of it. So "Mary had a little lamb" becomes: "AryMay adhay away ittlelay amblay." Now, write your very own coded message in Pig Latin to a friend, and read it aloud before you send it!

(004, English, Application, Originality)

FIVE, SIX, PICK UP STICKS

One, two, buckle my 22 pairs of shoes,

Three, four, go through 57 kinds of doors.

Five, six, watch 131 circus tricks

Seven, eight, has anyone told you that you look great?

Nine, ten, count the 85 military men,

Eleven, twelve, place 40 foods upon the shelves.

Thirteen, fourteen, brainstorm 8 items that are green,

Fifteen, sixteen, think of 19 things that could be keen.

Seventeen, eighteen, add the 60 parts of an acting scene.

Nineteen, twenty, count all the above items and yell, "Whee"!

(How many total items are there?)

(004, Mathematics, Problem Solving, Addition)

GA1415

THE LAND OF THE FIVE SENSES

Our five senses are extremely important to us. Without the sense of smell, sight, hearing, taste, and touch, we would be lost. We use each of our five senses every day we're alive. If we had to live without one of our senses, it would be extremely difficult to do the same things we are able to do today.

Design a brochure, taking us on a trip to the "Land of the Five Senses."

(004, English, Synthesis)

EGYPTIAN INFORMATION

Have you ever written to a foreign country for free posters, brochures, films, etc.? Are you interested in finding out more about a country like Egypt?

Well, all you need to do is to write to the following address, and ask for all the free information you would like to know about Egypt:

Tourist Information
630 Fifth Avenue
New York, NY 10020

When you receive the material(s), write a thank-you note and prepare a presentation to give to your class.

(004, Social Studies, Comprehension)

THE DUDE RANCH

The Baboon family of ten visited a dude ranch one spring,

Where they all rode horses that made them bounce and swing.

Eight others joined in with their vacation party,

The nights were festive and the food was hearty.

If 168 bananas were consumed by the troop,

And an equal number was eaten by each in the group.

How many bananas did each member eat,

Over the course of their vacation as an afternoon treat?

(005, Mathematics, Problem Solving, Division)

THE BIG FOUR

No such luck, what is that you say?

Your luck's been down, you're not OK?

Well try this out and hopefully you'll find,

Some brand-new luck and peace of mind!

Which countries are the really Big Four,

Who produces and sells the most goods, who makes more?

I'll give you a hint, the USA is one,

Find out the other three and then you'll be done!

(005, Social Studies, Knowledge)

GA1415

A HEARTY HOLIDAY

Valentine's Day comes every February 14th.

In highlighting the heart holiday, design a very special Valentine's Day commemorative stamp. Make it as big as your paper and don't forget the scalloped edges. Create as detailed a stamp as those you purchase.

(005, English, Synthesis)

HAPPY HERO

A high-strung hero of herpetology (study of reptiles and amphibians) hung out at a hospital harmonizing happily with himself, hiding out in a high chair only sixteen feet high. If every foot of height could hold thirty-three pounds of a hero, how many pounds could our hero have weighed to have still fit in the high chair?

(005, Mathematics, Problem Solving, Multiplication)

GA1415

SPLURGING WHILE SHOPPING

Mrs. Alvin and her grown-up daughter,
Went on a shopping spree one afternoon.
They covered a total of fifteen stores,
While listening to many a tune.
Stephanie bought three dresses at $10.99 apiece,
Mrs. Alvin came home with a new coat, $79.54.
The two also purchased a purse to share,
But the cost of $89.95 made their heads soar.
They stopped at the card shop rather hurriedly,
To choose cards and gifts for their men...
The total came to $42.76 at the register,
They bought very well for Tony and Ken.
The question of the day is the total,
That Mrs. Alvin and Stephanie spent that day.
While they splurged on their shopping spree,
On that hot and humid Thursday in May.

(How much total did they spend that day?)

(005, Mathematics, Problem Solving, Addition, Money)

PROBLEM SOLVING

An invention is simply a means to solve a problem or a new way of looking at something already in existence. Invent America out of Washington, D.C., looks at every school in the nation each year for the very best inventions constructed or thought of.

Invent a new way of folding a pair of socks.
Or invent a better fork.
Or invent a way to do your homework in a much better way.

(005, Social Studies, Synthesis)

GA1415

BROWN IN OUR TOWN

Brown is the color of chocolate or coffee and is the combination of black, red, and yellow. You can brown bag your lunch, have a brown belt in karate, or brown-nose your teacher. There are brown rice, brown rot, brown lung disease and brownies. Some brown-named animals consist of the brown bear, brown-tailed moth and brown trout. Brown sugar, Apple Brown Betty and brown bread are just a few brown culinary delights. Name five brown animals and five plants which contain hints of brown. Or state five likenesses and five differences between their physical properties in a chart. Or make something artistically creative out of a brown paper sack. Or state five differences between a Brownie and a Girl Scout, or a brownie and a cupcake.

Why do you think brown wood burns faster than green wood? Give five reasons to back up your hypothesis.

Or write a short story, comparing a brunette's life to that of a blonde's and answer the question, "Do blondes have more fun?"

(005, English, Synthesis)

TAKE PRIDE IN PRIDES

A pride of lions usually includes one male adult, three to five adult females, and ten to twenty cubs. Wherever the male journeys, the pride usually follows along.

If there are twenty prides in a 100-mile (161 km) radius, how many total number of lions is possible?

(005, Mathematics, Problem Solving, Multiplication)

THERE IS A SEASON

In Brazil there are no real seasons like we have in the United States, only the dry season and the wet season. During the wet season, heavy rains fall each day. During the dry season, it rains only once every few days. However, there is rain year-round off and on. Because it is so close to the equator, the temperatures remain very high.

Discover three countries whose weather behaves in the same way.

(005, Social Studies, Comprehension)

SPORT NUTS!

A sports diorama was held last week,
And many sports were tried, so to speak.
There were 15 very cold ice skaters,
Thirty-two girls were swimming laps by two's.
The roller skaters numbered 50,
And the 65 bowlers were big news!
The fishermen counted in at 21,
And the surfers measured in at 15.
The water skiers rounded out at 30,
And the 8 skateboarders looked pretty mean!
The golfers numbered a big 40,
While the baseball players had 17.
The question for you on this day,
 How many sports players were seen, OK?

(005, Mathematics, Problem Solving, Addition)

GA1415

SING ME A SONG

Ice cream is too good to be true! Almost everyone enjoys ice cream on special occasions or just as a delicious treat. Ice cream can be enjoyed both in summer and in winter and it is often used as a dessert, for example, pie ala mode.

Write the lyrics or words to an ice-cream song, set it to music, and sing it to your class! Start with a poem about ice cream, then think about a catchy tune and VIOLA! You've created your very own song!

(005, English, Synthesis, Originality)

MANY MOVIE MOMS

A multitude of macho movie mongers mesmerized millions at a mega-meeting of the "Mysteries of the Moon" marathon many Monday mornings ago. Megan's mother Mary, Martha's mother Margaret, Millicent's mama Myrtle, and Marcia's mammy Maria, all met at the Metro with the moon on their minds. Each mom bought ten meeting tickets and an extra one for her own mother.

If each ticket cost $7.50, what was the total charge for tickets that Monday morning in May?

(005, Mathematics, Problem Solving, Multiplication)

GA1415

A HORSE, OF COURSE!

There are many different breeds of horses, and just to mention some, the Appaloosa, Arabian, Morgan, Palamino, Pinto, Quarterhorse, and Thoroughbred. Each horse is unique in and of itself, and each has many fine characteristics. If you do a little research, perhaps you will discover what those endearing qualities might be.

Make a colorful foldout panel illustrating each of these types.

(005, Science, Application)

SKATER DUDES

John and Alex were the hottest skaters,

That ever had been seen in that town.

And if you weren't very careful,

They might accidentally run you down.

One day they started at the town of Queen's Point

And skated 14 minutes due west.

They then headed for 20 minutes towards north

To see if they were really and truly the best!

Another 50 minutes down south brought them to a complete stop,

Because standing right in front of them was a fully uniformed cop!

The only direction left for them to go was straight east,

The boys travelled for 80 minutes and then stopped in for a feast.

The question you are now asked in this inquiry,

Is the total amount of time John and Alex skated freely.

(005, Mathematics, Problem Solving, Time)

IVORY FOR SALE

Today the price of ivory is at an all-time high. Illegal hunting is a great threat to African elephants. Poachers use the tusks in trade for money or other items they desire.

Find a book that shows elephants with tusks. Use a picture of the elephant with tusks to model your sculpture after.

Sculpt out of clay a model of an African elephant with tusks.

(005, Science, Synthesis)

BASKETBALL FEVER

A total of 732 players tried out for the team,

Quite a lot for basketball it surely would seem.

To be a superstar was every boy's dream,

But only 12 would make it, came the coach's scream!

At the tryouts, 3 baskets were shot by every boy,

The way they handled the ball you'd have thought it was a toy.

Each kid made a basket from far, far away.

 Your job?

To pick out all the baskets that were shot that day!

(005, Mathematics, Problem Solving, Multiplication)

44

CURRENCY MARKS

In Mexico, the currency used is the peso. In Italy, the currency is a lire. In France, they use francs. Deutch marks are the currency used in Germany.

Try to discover what form of currency is used in each of the following countries: U.S.S.R., China, India, Sweden, Switzerland, Australia, Canada, Denmark, Brazil, Japan, Iceland and Scotland.

(005, Social Studies, Knowledge)

MODERN DAY ROBIN HOOD

Once upon a time, lived a rich Russian spy...
Who was ordered to recover secret papers and try to fly
Off to another country and over to the West,
Where many Russians believed truly was the best.
Well Vladmir knew the plans like the back of his hand,
For he was one of the best spies ever in the land.
He robbed the Kremlin right out in the broad daylight,
And the robbery was successful—not a single solitary fright.
He stole not only secret papers, but ten bags of loot as well,
And in each of the bags, a beautiful brooch which he could sell.
The brooches were worth $1505.00 apiece you see,
And once he sold them he did finally cease with glee.
Stealing from the rich and giving to many more,
Just exactly how much did Vladmir donate to the poor?

(005, Mathematics, Problem Solving, Multiplication)

GA1415

SEAL-A-RIFIC

There are eighteen different kinds of seals, such as the Wedell, harbor seals, elephant seals, and fur seals. These seals live in different parts of the oceans, and thousands can live together at one time. Seals are very interesting creatures and if you do a little research on them, hopefully you will find this out too.

On a poster, illustrate five of the eighteen types of seals and write a brief description under each.

(005, Science, Application)

RAINBOW POETRY

Rainbow poetry involves choosing one or more colors of the rainbow, brainstorming all the things in the world that are one or more of those colors, and then writing a poem using as many of those words as possible.

Your job is to write a rainbow or color poem. For example, things that are *green*— plants, lime, lettuce, cabbage, sea, spring, frog, moss, peas, Martians and money. An example poem for green:

Plants have ants, and limes are green,
The spring has sprung, now what a scene!
Peas are crunchy, and moss is mushy,
Money is cash, and cabbage is squshy.
Martians are little and green and petite,
Frogs can croak, and are fun to eat.
The sea is green and so is a lettuce head,
When something's green in my fridge, it might be dead.
Your job today is to make a list,
Of all green things, I do insist.

(005, English, Fluency, Originality, Synthesis)

GA1418

AT THE MOVIES

You're a movie critic and your job is right here,

Review five movies and make sure your reviews are clear.

Actors, actresses, unique scenes running through,

Special effects, sound effects, and...

Plot must be included too.

When you have concluded and your review is complete,

Take yourself out and buy yourself a big fat treat!

(005, Social Studies, Evaluation)

BICYCLE ACCESSORIES

Everyone's choice for a bicycle is different. That is why bicycle shops carry a wide variety of bicycles. If you will notice all the different bicycles in the racks at your school, you will see the great number of differently made bicycles that there truly are in existence today. Bicycle accessories have also taken on a whole new look; the Spandex pants, helmet, gloves, lights, water containers, and coin carriers are just some of the equipment bikers use to go riding and racing.

Write a TV commercial or jingle to advertise a new line of bicycle accessories. (Make up or design the line of bicycle accessories yourself.)

(005, English, Synthesis)

LIGHTHEARTED LIMERICKS

A limerick is a special kind of poem with an aabba rhyme scheme. For example:

There once was a man named Tony Tell,

Who made a wish in his wishing well.

The coin went down first,

But it must have been cursed,

Because Tell leaned over and he fell.

Write three limericks on topics of your choice.

(005, English, Synthesis)

EARLY PROBLEMS

In the beginning of time, early animals had three main problems: standing up, breathing, and staying wet inside.

List some of the problems our modern day animals must endure.

(005, Science, Comprehension)

GA14

SOMETHING OR NOTHING?

Sometimes it is better to have nothing of something rather than something of anything. For instance, it is better to have no D's or F's on your report card than to have some, and it is better to have no enemies than to have even one.

Brainstorm twenty things in life that it is better to have "none of" rather than "some of."

(005, Social Studies, Fluency)

SOCIETY'S BIGGEST PROBLEM

Drug abuse is said to be one of the biggest, if not THE biggest problem plaguing our society today.

Take the theme of "Drugs" and list all the pros and cons of their possible use. Take a position for or against drug usage and list all of your reasons in a position paper.

(005, Science, Evaluation)

GA1415

TELEPHONE TALK

Telephones have become vastly important in our lives today. Take the letters in the word *telephones* and make as many little words as possible out of them. Example: teen

(005, English, Analysis, Fluency)

WHO'S THE BEST?

Seventeen brainy professors were studying up for a test,

They actually wanted to determine which one was truly best.

The test took a total of three long hours,

Each one's forehead looked like it had rained showers.

If each of the questions measured three minutes long,

How many total questions were played without a song?

(005, Mathematics, Problem Solving, Time)

GA14

HOLIDAY HAVEN

The United States celebrates many different holidays: New Year's, Easter, Thanksgiving, Halloween and Christmas, just to name a few. Other countries celebrate their own holidays as well.

Your job is to create a new holiday, complete with name, what is to be celebrated, what special activities or events are to be held, what special foods are eaten, whether or not there should be a parade, and what kinds of decorations are needed, etc.

(005, Social Studies, Synthesis)

SUPER STRIDES

A walking giraffe can take strides of fifteen feet (4.5 m) long. That doesn't mean that he always will go that far each stride, but he has the potential to go that far if he so chooses.

If there were three giraffes walking through the jungle for one mile (1.61 km), how many total strides would that be if the giraffe took his longest strides?

(Hint: There are 5280 feet in one mile.)

(005, Mathematics, Problem Solving, Measurement)

GA1415

FLIP-FLOPS STARTLE SHOPS

Some commonly used flip-flop words consist of abba-dabba, bow-wow, chit-chat, click-clack, ding-a-ling, flip-flop, hanky-panky, mumbo-jumbo, pitter-patter, rub-dub, super-duper, tick-tock, walkie-talkie, and zigzag, just to mention a few.

Use these flip-flop words to write a creative story entitled "The Super-Duper, Ticky-Tacky, Walkie-Talkie."

(005, English, Synthesis, Originality)

WONDERS OF THE WORLD

There are many different wonders of the world, including the Great Pyramids in Egypt, and the Grand Canyon in Arizona. There are ancient, natural, and modern wonders, and these incorporate many different truly remarkable landmarks around the world.

Create a mobile which depicts hand-drawn pictures of at least five of these wonders. Use 5" x 8" (12.7 x 20.32 cm) index cards on which to draw the pictures, string to hang them on, and a hanger to attach them all together.

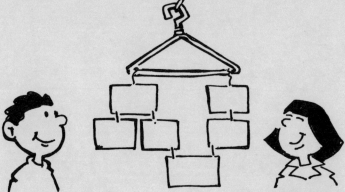

(005, Social Studies, Synthesis, Originality)

GA1415

WALL BALL

The Great Wall of China is the only man-made structure that can be seen by astronauts on the moon. The Berlin Wall was torn down during the social changes at the end of the 1980's by the East German government.

Try and discover all that you can about each of these two walls. Then compare and contrast them for all their similarities and differences.

(005, Social Studies, Analysis)

CONCRETE POETRY

Concrete poetry is poetry written in the shape of the topic being written about. For example, a poem about baseball might be written in the shape of a bat and ball. Or one written about fishing might be in the shape of a person using a pole and catching a fish.

Write three concrete poems about three of your favorite subjects. Make your poems large enough so they are easy to read.

(005, English, Synthesis)

GA1415

AN AIRLINE TICKET TO WHERE?

Many people take trips to other states or countries. In order to do so, most use airplanes for at least part of their travel. Have you ever thought about what kinds of information are needed on an airline ticket?

Research this question, and then create a simulated airline ticket to the one spot in the world you would most like to travel to. Include a statement why.

(006, Social Studies, Synthesis)

INTO THE BEYOND

Space travel is one of man's greatest dreams–to be able to search the galaxy, and explore what lies beyond.

Display at least five different space vehicles on a poster, and label their component parts. Write a comparison-contrast essay citing similarities and differences between two of the five.

(006, Science, Analysis, Synthesis)

GA1415

POTPOURRI OF MATHEMATICS

12 + 20 and forty plus fifteen,

I love the colors blue and green.

8 - four and sixty - 3,

One potato, two potato, I've got you on my knee.

6 x thirteen and 33 x forty-four,

Rah! Rah! Go team and give 'em some more!

One hundred twenty-six divided by 3 and 147 divided by two,

If you can do lines 1, 3, 5 and 7,

I've got to hand it to you!

(006, Mathematics, Problem Solving, Addition, Subtraction, Multiplication, Division)

BICYCLE BANTER

Riding a bicycle can be quite an experience, especially the few times you've taken a bad fall!

Compose a series of poems about bicycle riding and combine them into your very own poetry book entitled "The Spokes on You!"

Every time you tri(cycle),
To hastily ride your bi(cycle)…
Uni(eed) (you need) to stop and sigh,
Or else wave bye-bye!

(006, English, Synthesis)

GA1415

ADDING NUMBERS

One, two, three, four,

Fears we can't ignore.

Five, six, seven, eight,

Rules we have to rate.

Nine, ten, eleven, twelve,

Thoughts we have to bank and shelve.

Thirteen, fourteen, fifteen, sixteen,

Rooms we have to clean.

Seventeen, eighteen, nineteen, twenty,

About our fun? We have plenty!

If you add each number above,

You'll have a total that would fill a glove!

(006, Mathematics, Problem Solving, Addition)

BE ALL THAT YOU CAN BE!

"Coke is it!" "Pepsi–the choice of a new generation." "Cos and Affect" (Bill Cosby). "Be all that you can be!" (Army). "Double your pleasure, double your fun!" (Wrigley's Doublemint). "How do you spell RELIEF?" (Rolaids). "If you care enough to send the very best, send Hallmark." These are some of the most popular slogans of the 1980's and '90's.

Create a new product and write a catchy original jingle for it. Design a billboard ad to go with it.

(006, English, Synthesis, Originality)

GA1415

PHENOMENAL PYRAMIDS

One of the Seven Wonders of the Ancient World just happens to be the Egyptian pyramids which are located near Cairo, Egypt, at Giza.

Imagine having none of our modern day technological equipment and just having to lift over two million separate blocks of limestone! Write down twenty of the most imaginative ways one might accomplish this feat!

(006, Science, Problem Solving, Fluency)

AN ELEPHANT STAMPEDE

Eighty elephants trampled into the African town,

They destroyed forty buildings that went down, down, down!

Luckily they were soon visited by a very famous clown,

Who raised money on their behalf and many lost their frown.

On that same day a lion in shades of tan and brown,

Attacked a beautiful lady in a long studded gown.

Now if each of the animals did $500 worth of destruction,

How much total will be needed for the town's reconstruction?

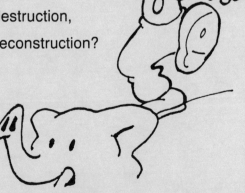

(006, Mathematics, Problem Solving, Multiplication)

GA1415

JAPANESE HAIKU

Haiku is Japanese poetry written about nature in three lines, with five syllables on the first line, seven syllables on the second line, and five syllables on the third line. For example:

> Rainbow arching low
> Colors bright and beautiful
> Easy on the eye

You are to write two haikus; one is to be about animals (any you choose) and the other is to be about plants (again, any you choose).

(006, English, Synthesis, Originality)

ACUPUNCTURE

In China, acupuncture is a common way of treating patients medically. More recently, many Americans are using acupuncture to cure their aches and pains as well. As a matter of fact, many pain clinics in the United States use acupuncture as one of their main pain killers.

Research what this type of medicine is, how it works, and how widely it is practiced in the United States.

(006, Social Studies, Knowledge)

SPEAK YOUR MIND

Bicycles have now become a frequently used method of transportation as well as a popular means of exercise. You are sick and tired of the fact that there is nowhere on the streets to ride your bike and you're afraid of getting hurt.

Write a proposal to your City Council, encouraging them to include more bicycle paths on city streets.

(006, Social Studies, Application)

RAZZMATAZZ!

Back in the days of the street gang,

In a back alley where they would hang, (out, that is!)

They played some great jazz,

About thirty were razzmatazz,

And the guy who collected the money was Fang!

If on a certain day in May one year,

The street gang collected $93.30 without fear.

How much was each jazz song worth,

To the gang who called themselves "Rebirth"?

(006, Mathematics, Problem Solving, Division)

GA1415

BIRDS WERE THERE, TOO!

During the dinosaur age, many different birds evolved as well. For instance, the pterosaur was a winged and toothless reptile who may have hung upside down from distant cliffs along the ocean side. A pteranodon was believed to be the largest pterosaur, with a wingspan of 24 feet (7.2 m) and a body the size of a goose.

Research this period in time and make a list and description for each of the birds that existed at the same time as the dinosaurs.

(006, Science, Knowledge)

SAY IT WITH A CARD

Hallmark and American Greetings, just to name two, are greeting card companies making millions of dollars on their cards each year. As you may have noticed when you've gone to purchase a card, some of the greetings are extremely clever and some are not.

Design a birthday card for your worst enemy, your best friend, and a family member. Include catchy verses.

(006, English, Synthesis, Originality)

GA1

MR. FROGGIE

Frogs are attracted to different plants in the ponds where they live. And because they are green they blend right in with their surroundings.

Create a game where Mr. Froggie is in search of the perfect lily pad. Use a file folder, index cards, brads, markers, envelopes, and glue. Use as many details as possible.

(006, Science, Synthesis, Originality, Elaboration)

AIR-BOUND?

If you shot a cannon ball straight up into the air at a speed of 100 mph (161 kmph), would it ever stop before it hit the ground? Give up?

You bet it would! For about one-tenth of a second before it started to come down.

Now, if a total of 360 cannon balls were shot out of the same cannon over the course of one year, how much total time would there be when all the balls were stopped in midair?

(006, Mathematics, Problem Solving, Multiplication)

GA1415

SALUTE TO PICASSO

Picasso was one of the most abstract painters of our century (1900's). Not only did he paint really unusual paintings, but he also created some truly unique sculptures. In addition to sculptures, watercolors and oils, he worked with cubism and fragmentation or distortion of the human body and other items in nature.

Locate one of Picasso's works in a library book and criticize or complement the painting or sculpture in a salute to Picasso.

(006, English, Analysis)

THE TOY INDUSTRY

Children's toys are BIG BUSINESS! Imagine a toy that you have wanted for a very long time. You bugged and bugged your parents until you got it, right? Now imagine that every other child in America did the exact same thing! Can you see how toys can be really big business?

Write and illustrate a newspaper advertisement for a new kind of children's toy which you invent yourself. Place a price tag on it too!

(006, Social Studies, Synthesis, Originality)

GA14

A SIGN OF COURAGE

In the Arctic, hunting a polar bear is a sign of courage. If you were faced with this challenge, what method of conquest would you choose? Would it be a bow and arrow, a gun, a knife, an axe, etc.?

Write a one-page thriller explaining your ideas. Concentrate more on the slyness and cunning you would show in trying to outwit the polar bear rather than on the violence of the kill.

(006, Science, Synthesis, Originality)

SHE WAS PAID HER DUE

Once upon a time lived a girl named Sue,

Who hadn't a single thing left to do,

She had done twenty-seven really good deeds,

Like cleaning furniture and cutting down weeds,

At fifty cents per deed she was paid her due.

How much total cash did Sue earn this day, say you?

(006, Mathematics, Problem Solving, Multiplication, Decimals)

SHAKE AND BAKE

If you ever cook a cake,
Just make sure you shake and bake,
If you're ever in a huge earthquake,
Reach for cover for your sake.
If endowed with a bad toothache,
Call the dentist when you wake,
If you know someone really is a fake,
Just give him some marbles and see what he'll make.
If in your garden, you find a snake,
Get out quickly your very best rake.
If you have a secret plan to undertake,
Complete it fast–you've got a lot at stake.
Take any three-letter word ending,
Like -ite, -ail, or -air,
And brainstorm a list of same-sounding words,
To help you write a poem without nary a care.

(006, English, Synthesis, Originality)

JANGLE A JINGLE

There are many different types of advertising including Yellow Pages, newspapers, magazines, billboards, radio, and television. Each of these types of advertising helps to sell products to the general public. If we didn't have advertising, no one would know what products were available.

Compose a jingle (song) for an advertisement about a new kind of gum, and invent the gum yourself!

(006, Social Studies, Synthesis)

GA14

TEENY TINY BABIES

Koalas are only about the size of bumblebees when they are born. In comparison to other Australian baby marsupials, a small koala will spend his early life growing in and out of his mother's pouch. As he gets older, he will leave the pouch and venture onto his mother's back. Finally, he will learn to climb trees and be out on his own.

List all of the animals of comparable size when they are full-grown as the size of the baby koalas.

(006, Science, Fluency)

WILLIE'S NIGHT OUT

A fish named Willie was a bass,
And he loved to blow his instrument made of brass.
One day right in the middle of his class,
He wondered if he was ever going to pass!
There just happened to be a nice and friendly lass,
Whom he met later for a swim next to the grass.
Someone was staring at them through the glass,
And Willie's girlfriend began to sass.
Soon there was such a wide-scale mass,
That Willie got in his car and went for gas!

You are to figure out this fact:
If Willie spent 4 hours and 33 minutes with his lass,
And they began their night together at 1:09,
What time was it when Willie went for gas?
And, if it took him 17 minutes to gas up for good,
What time was it when he returned to the neighborhood?

(006, Mathematics, Problem Solving, Time)

65

THE ZEBRA—BLACK OR WHITE STRIPES?

Some believe that a zebra's stripes help it to hide or camouflage itself within the herd. Others believe the stripes draw attention to it by predators. No one is really sure since we haven't quite figured out all of nature yet.

Are zebras white animals with black stripes or black animals with white stripes? Research the *Zebra Zoobook* or the encyclopedia for the answer. Write a short-answer essay revealing the facts.

(006, Science, Knowledge)

FROGS AND FELINES FIGHT!

Fifty-five freaking frogs forced forty-four furry felines to fight fourteen ferocious finches for feathers. If each frog and each feline found four feathers from each finch, how many total feathers would that be?

(006, Mathematics, Problem Solving, Multiplication)

GA14

A WEB OF STORY PROBLEMS

For Halloween, design a large spider's web out of cardboard, yarn, string, tacks, nails or any other suitable materials which will hold story problems that you create and write on index cards yourself. Try to include as many of your classmate's names as possible while writing the problems. Everyone likes to hear his name, and what better way to get the whole class involved!

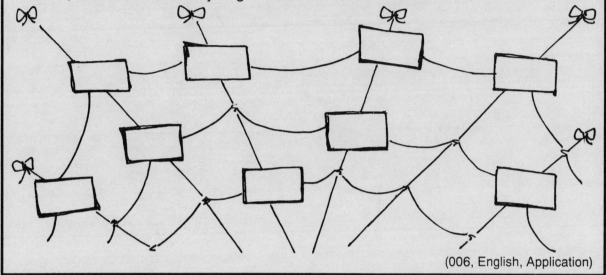

(006, English, Application)

DELVE INTO THE BOOKS!

Here are a few questions for you to research,

Get out the encyclopedia and begin to search.

Which countries produce the very most steel?

Which countries mine coal, at the top of each deal?

Which countries produce the top oil amounts?

So they can put cash in their many bank accounts?

Where does most natural gas come from?

Answer these questions and you won't feel dumb!

(006, Social Studies, Knowledge)

RAND, THE DONKEY

A while ago a donkey named Rand,

Decided to really stand up and take a stand!

He rode fourteen laps tremendously fast,

So that he was sure he wouldn't be last,

And when he came in first, it was grand!

If each lap took 22.5 minutes to go,

How much total time did Rand really flow?

(006, Mathematics, Problem Solving, Decimals, Multiplication)

GREEN IS THE COLOR

Green is the color of growing grass, don't you know?
And all those green plants—well they just grow and grow!
Spinach, lettuce, turnip tops and much, much more,
Can all be bought at your local green grocery store!
There are bowling greens and golf greens,
And folding green and green with envy.
You can be green-eyed, or in a green field,
Where the marching band refuses to yield!
Green cards and green dragons are very hard to find,
Green mold and green monkeys really stagger the mind.
The Green River and green room give others quite a look,
And a green thumbless person means you've definitely been took!

Define *green* in a poem of your very own choosing,
Or create a green monster, one distinguished, refined and divine.
Or compile five fun things centering around green,
Or design green invitations for a holiday dance so fine.

(006, English, Synthesis, Originality)

GA1419

INSTITUTING IDIOMS

An idiom is a figure of speech which has a meaning as a whole that may not be suggested by its parts. For instance, if Sally says, "Sal's driving me up the wall," the literal or true meaning would be that Sal is actually in a car driving Sally up the wall of a building. As an idiom it means "Sal really irritates me."

Many of the expressions that we use mean something else. You are to think of and illustrate at least three different idioms of your choice. Don't write the idiom under the drawing, write it on the back. That way you can quiz your classmates, teacher and parents to see if they can figure out the idiom you drew.

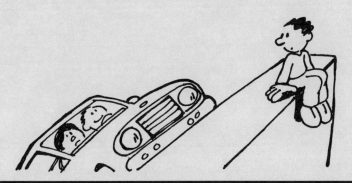

(006, English, Application)

BIOGRAPHICAL POEM

You've all heard of a biography. It is a story written about an individual written by another person. Well, a biographical poem is a poem written about a person by another author or poet.

You are to choose any famous individual in history and write a sixteen-line biographical poem about his or her life and achievements. Be sure to include as much as you can about his or her life so whoever reads the poem will know as much about the person as you have learned. Have fun!

(006, Social Studies, Synthesis, Originality)

GA1415

ONE CENT FOR THE SCENT YOU SENT

Homonyms are words that sound the same but may be spelled differently and definitely mean different things. Some most commonly used pairs or trios of homonyms include aisle, I'll, isle; allowed, aloud; ate, eight; cent, scent, sent; deer, dear; do, dew; gnu, knew, new; hear, here; idle, idol, idyll; knight, night; main, Maine, mane; peace, piece; road, rowed, rode; tail, tale; toe, tow; vain, vane, vein; week, weak. Use some of these in a homonym poem of twelve lines or more. Try to make the poem as funny and detailed as possible.

(006, English, Synthesis, Originality, Elaboration)

I WANT TO BE LEFT ALONE!

Imagine that a skunk was in your front yard! How would you ever get rid of it before it sprayed you? Actually, a skunk will only spray its scent when it feels cornered and can't escape. But first it will warn you by jumping on its front feet, humping its back, and hissing! This may be the skunk's way of letting you know that it wants you to leave it alone!

What are some ways humans have of letting others know they want to be left alone? Make a list!

(006, Social Studies, Comprehension, Fluency)

GA1415

OUR WILDLIFE MAY SOON BE GONE!

Many endangered species are all around us and if we don't start preserving our wildlife, there soon won't be any left. Some examples of threatened wildlife include the African chimpanzee, Bolivian chinchilla, American crocodile, Madagascarian forest-dwelling lemur, and the North American whooping crane.

Imagine that all these animals lived in one big zoo. Design what the zoo looks like and what each animal's enclosure should include.

(006, Science, Synthesis, Originality)

PENGUINS FIND GOLD

The two penguins sat out in the cold,
Wondering just what it was that made them so bold.
They had just discovered 630 pounds of gold,
In the ice and under the fold.
They sent out a survey and polled…
One hundred ten penguins, then put them on hold.
It was later discovered the gold had been "stoled,"
After it was wrapped up and then carefully rolled.
Now the question at hand at this time,
And you must answer it or it'll be a crime…
What percent of the gold did they keep,
If fourteen pounds was what each did reap?

(006, Mathematics, Multiplication, Division, Percent)

71

IT'S DINNERTIME!

Before a koala sits down to eat its dinner, he takes a big sniff. Why do you think he does this?

Check your answer out in a topic book which focuses on koalas. Try to discover also all about the koala's eating habits, mating habits, how Mama takes care of the young, etc.

(006, Science, Comprehension)

AN HERB OF THE CARROT FAMILY?

Celery is a European herb of the carrot family. Can you believe that?

Imagine that celery stalks could grow to be 18 feet (5.4 m) tall? What are some new uses you can discover for these gigantic stalks? Make a list!

(006, Science, Problem Solving, Fluency)

GA1415

IT'S A BIRD!
IT'S A PLANE!
NO, IT'S A FISH!

Ever heard of a fish called a mudskipper? Well, it accomplishes an amazing feat! Every day it crawls out of the water on its fins!

Name as many animals as you can think of who have adapted parts of their bodies to accomplish unusual feats.

(006, Science, Knowledge)

A DINOSAUR DOES GOOD!

A smart-witted dinosaur was making plans,

One bright and sunny May day.

He started thinking about Disneyland,

And all the different things he could play!

He decided on 16 rides to begin his trail,

And went for a walk with Mickey to get the mail,

Next he bought toys for all of his 13 friends,

And asked himself, "Does this fun never end?"

If each ride costs $1.25 and each toy $4.50,

How much money did the dinosaur spend in a jiffy?

(006, Mathematics, Problem Solving, Addition, Money)

GA1415

A RACING RIOT

As the car race began and the flag came down,

The festivities had begun and each racer was renowned.

After going around the track at 190 mph,

It was noticed atop one of the cars were one hundred five-pound bags of flour.

The bags of flour fell at the rate of two per minute...

To add excitement to the race, as long as they weren't in it!

The question of the day is to figure out this without stop,

If the race lasted forty-five minutes, how many bags of flour were left on top?

How many total pounds of flour fell and went flop?

(007, Mathematics, Problem Solving, Multiplication, Subtraction)

ENDANGERED SPECIES EVERYWHERE

Animals come in many shapes, sizes and colors, but no one even knows how many kinds of animals there are since no one has been able to count them all!

We know there are millions of different animals, but each year hundreds of new ones are being found. In addition, some of the animals that have been here for a long time have become extinct, which means they no longer exist.

In zoos, wildlife conservation is one of the main goals, and in some cases the only means against extinction of which they are aware.

Research wildlife conservation and write down all the ways the conservationists are trying to save endangered species.

(007, Science, Comprehension)

GA1415

IT'S A PARTY!

You're at a party and the music is loud,
The folks are boogying and there is quite a crowd.
Board games are being played in the living room,
And in the kitchen they're playing hula with a broom.
Attending are 47 kids who each brought two good friends,
Of those, 20 sat in the fish tank and suddenly got the bends.
Three girls had to be taken away in an ambulance.
They cut their legs jumping on the fence and didn't have a chance.
All of a sudden, 13 more cars arrived, each carrying 4,
They had come to the party but the others were out the door.
The party moved to the backyard and the neighbors came over then,
Five houses of 5 joined in for fun and stayed until who knows when.
When the party finally ended late into the night,
How many total attended and were there in plain sight?

(007, Mathematics, Problem Solving, Addition, Multiplication)

JUMBO JUNK

Old packages, used cups, dented-in soda cans, crinkled wrappers, twisted ties, empty bottles, soiled tissues, pieces of hair, boxes with one little morsel left, stale milk cartons, and crumpled meat papers are just a few of the things that could be found in one's garbage pail.

Complete a trash can poem which focuses on at least five different pieces of garbage found in a trash can.

(007, English, Synthesis)

75

GA1415

A BICYCLE BUILT FOR TWO

Have you ever seen a bicycle built for two? It's a pretty rare view, isn't it? Imagine seeing twenty tandems coming toward you down the street! A pretty awesome sight, eh?

Create an adventure story about Barry and Bobby, the twin brothers who ride a bicycle built for two in a race all over your town. Do they win? Something very strange occurs during the race. What is it? How does the whole story finish?

(007, English, Synthesis, Originality)

BOUGHT AND SOLD!

If you bought a skateboard for $10.00, sold it to Allen for $20.00, bought it back for $30.00, sold it to Jake for $40.00, bought it back for $60.00, and finally sold it to Steve for $90.00, would you lose money or make money? How much?

(007, Mathematics, Problem Solving, Addition, Subtraction)

GA14

ZOOM INTO A ZOO!

Zoos have changed quite a bit over the past one hundred years. Many zoos are dispensing with cages and using natural habitat enclosures instead. Habitat includes giving an animal air, water, space, and shelter.

Predict and make a model of what a zoo will look like in the year 3000.

(007, Science, Evaluation, Originality)

AUTOBIOGRAPHICAL POEM

An autobiography is a story written about a person by the person himself. An autobiographical poem is also written about the person by the person himself but written in poetic verse.

Make a list of four things that happened to you during each year of your life and write one four-line stanza about yourself for every year you've been alive! VOILA! Your very own autobiographical poem!

Example:

When I was only two, I believe,
I used to wipe my nose on my sleeve.
I once fell out of a tree, it's true,
And all of this happened at the age of two.

(007, English, Synthesis)

NEWSPAPER CREATIONS

A newspaper can present happenings from your city, state, country and even from around the world. If you ever get a chance, you should pick one up and read an article about something which interests you.

Use a newspaper to design something creative and imaginative and that also has to do with some article in that particular issue. You can create a sculpture, a model, or a picture. Use paints to add hints of color on the finished product.

(007, Social Studies, Synthesis)

EXCELLENT EXPONENTS

Everyone loves big numbers, especially when describing how much they'd like to win in the lottery. Well, rather than writing out all those zeros, there's a much easier way! Use exponents, which is a way to tell how many times to multiply the base or main number by itself. 10^3 reads ten to the power of 3, and it means 10 x 10 x 10 or a one with three zeros, or 1000.

10^6 reads 10 to the power of 6 or 10 x 10 x 10 x 10 x 10 x 10 or 1,000,000.

Figure out the following powers of ten and what each number is called. Try using the encyclopedia for help.

$10^9 =$ $10^{12} =$ $10^{15} =$ $10^{27} =$ $10^{33} =$ $10^{42} =$

$10^{18} =$ $10^{21} =$ $10^{24} =$ $10^{54} =$ $10^{60} =$ $10^{100} =$

(007, Mathematics, Exponents)

GA14

PUPPETRY

Puppets come in many shapes and sizes. Wouldn't you enjoy making a creative puppet yourself?

Take a piece of butcher paper and roll it up. Tape and turn it into a creative puppet by cutting into the top for hair and gluing on a face, as well as other features. Be really imaginative and add yarn, colored fadeless art paper, pipe cleaners, feathers, and any other things you can think of. Name your puppet and give it a personality. Put on a puppet show.

(007, English, Synthesis)

A DIAMOND SHINES AND MINES

Mining is a very important industry which takes minerals from the ground. There are many different types of mining, not the least of which is mining for diamonds.

Research the various types of mining and write an informational one to two-page report.

(007, Social Studies, Analysis)

GA1415

JUMP INTO THIS!

On land, the frog's muscular hind legs are used for jumping. In some parts of the country, frog jumping contests are big business. But some people feel that frog jumping is inhumane to the frogs. What do you think?

Compose a play about the three frogs who jumped their way to fame.

(007, Science, Synthesis)

A PARADOX

1. You are not a student. 2. You are the only person who will read this problem. 3. You do not go to school. 4. Numbers 1, 2, 3 and 4 are all false.

Well, you are a student so that is false. You aren't the only one who will read this problem. You do go to school so this is false also. But if number 4 is true, and numbers 1, 2 and 3 are false, then numbers 1, 2 and 3 are true *and* false at the same time. This is called a paradox.

Paradoxes make you think about statements and make you question what you think is one way but really is another. It takes a lot of intense thinking to totally figure out a paradox. See if you can write one.

(007, Mathematics, Problem Solving, Synthesis)

GA14

CONSTRUCT A CONTRAPTION

Inventions are described as something thought up or mentally fabricated such as a new device or method of doing something. When we are combining something, two or more things together, we are synthesizing and that takes a lot of thinking.

Combine a tricycle, a skateboard, and a hot air balloon and draw your new contraption. Give a detailed description of your invention, and make sure it has a name.

(007, Social Studies, Synthesis, Originality)

CROCORIDDLES

A bird called an Egyptian plover will never be eaten by a crocodile–not even when it walks right into the crocodile's mouth! The reason for this is because the plover helps to keep the crocodile's mouth and teeth clean!

Write ten riddles about crocodiles, alligators, and plovers. For example: What's green and black and red all over? An alligator who just rubbed against the evening newspaper.

(007, Science, Synthesis)

GA1415

FLASH!

In photography, there are many terms which are necessary to know. In a "Photography Extra News Clip," define the following: negative, prints, developing, lens, safelight, underexposed, shutter, panning, iris, diaphragm, aperture, control system, depth of field, focus control, and film cartridge. Then use all of those terms in a short photography essay.

(007, Social Studies, Knowledge)

LISTEN TO THE HEARTBEAT

We've been heartfelt, heartbroken, hard-hearted, heart-free, heart-stricken, hearty, heartsick; had heart-to-heart talks, heartthrobs, heartburn, heartache, and felt heartbeats. Well, the average person's heart beats 103,680 times a day. How many times is this per hour? Per minute?

Ask an adult to show you how to find your pulse rate and compare your beats per minute to the average person above.

(007, Mathematics, Problem Solving, Division, Time)

GA1

DOES THE EARLY BIRD GET THE WORM?

"The early bird gets the worm." What does this mean in terms of man?

Write a short oral report which explains this statement, and share it with the class. Cite as many examples as possible where this statement is applicable to our society.

(007, English, Application, Synthesis)

ASH REVISITED

There once was a little boy named FLASH,
Who wanted to earn a lot of extra CASH,
He found out a way that he could MASH,
A hundred barrels worth $100.00 apiece filled with ASH.
Unfortunately, one of the barrels did CRASH,
And FLASH was paid only one-fourth of his STASH.
He left the company, off in a DASH,
To go to a restaurant and eat corned beef HASH.
The hash cost $2.49 and the waiter was BRASH,
And FLASH threw his HASH right into the TRASH!
Being in a hurry and really quite RASH,
FLASH wore an outfit that truly did CLASH!
He noticed on his left arm a GASH,
Where he had hit his shoe and had a SMASH.

The question you need to solve today,
Is how much FLASH had from his last pay...
After buying that HASH that he threw in the TRASH,
Now, what is FLASH'S total spending CASH?

(007, Mathematics, Problem Solving, Multiplication, Division, Subtraction)

LIE AWAY!

You've been told all your life not to tell lies and that lying is wrong. Well, about 99 percent of the time, that is true—lying is wrong! But every once in a great while, you are told that it's all right to lie. And now is one of those times!

You are to write the most extraordinary lie you can possibly think of! And not only that, but you are to write this lie in the form of a ten-line humorous poem. VOILA! A poetic lie! Have fun!

(007, English, Synthesis, Elaboration)

NUCLEAR ENERGY—GOOD OR BAD?

Did you know that one ton (.9 t) of nuclear fuel, uranium, can produce as much energy as 30,000 tons (27,000 t) of coal? The top world producers of uranium include Canada, U.S.A., South Africa and France.

How do you feel about the nuclear issue? Should nuclear power plants be allowed or banned forever? Write a position paper expressing your views.

(007, Social Studies, Evaluation)

GA1415

RHYMING MADNESS

If you ever use flies as bait,
Tell us just how they really rate.
If you notice a little bad trait,
Try hard not to recognize it or to hate.
If ever you have a friend named Kate,
Excuse her if she's a little late,
If you ever have to spend time and wait,
Make sure you have someone validate.
If you need to do a verb conjugate,
It helps if you precisely indicate.
When looking for the perfect animal mate,
Make certain the two try to relate.
If unclear whether a spy will infiltrate,
Just send out a possible date.
And if you believe that something is fate,
Just head out for the nearest gate.

Take any two-or-three-letter word ending,
Like *-ish*, *-oar*, or *-um*, and write lots of them...
And incorporate them into a brilliant poem.

(007, English, Synthesis)

MONEY–MOOLA!

Money is very important in our society, and some people believe money can even buy happiness.

Brainstorm a list of ten things you would want to do if suddenly you won the lottery!

(007, Social Studies, Fluency)

THE MUSIC TO WHICH THE COBRA DANCES

Have you ever heard that the cobra dances to the music of the snake charmer's pipe? The cobra can't hear the music and when its basket is opened, it rises in defense and then follows the movement of the pipe, not because it is responding to the music.

Find out all you can about a cobra and other similar snakes. Are there any misconceptions about which we might be interested? Write a one-page summary of your findings.

(007, Science, Comprehension)

CONSECUTIVE NUMBERS

Consecutive numbers are all those numbers which are in a row and always in chronological order. For example, 8 and 9 are consecutive numbers and so are 4 and 5. Think of all the trios of numbers or sets which equal 6, 9, 15, 30, 33, 50, and 90.

Now find other pairs of numbers which will also, when added, equal the sums above.

(007, Mathematics, Problem Solving, Consecutive Numbers)

A SWISS TRAVEL ARTICLE

Switzerland is a small European country covered over half by the Alps and the Jura Mountains. Switzerland has long celebrated a tradition of neutrality and freedom.

Write an article on a trip to Switzerland for a travel magazine including clothes, fashion, equipment needed for the trip, type of housing available, food, recreation, time and method of travel, and overall possible cost. Use all resources available to you—magazines, books, encyclopedia, travel agency, etc.

(007, Social Studies, Application)

THE BEST OF THE BEST

You've been told you're "the best,"

The best in the whole wide west! (or east)

And with the best comes some responsibility, too,

When you're the best, no one else will do things for you.

Brainstorm a list of fifteen reasons why…

You truly are the best and are flying to the sky,

When you have finished and think you're really done,

Try going up to twenty and reaching for the sun!

(007, English, Fluency)

GA1415

ELEPHANT STAMP(EDE)

Many of China's and India's stamps display beautiful elephant pictures. Stamp collecting is a wonderful hobby to have and all you need is the price of a stamp to purchase a mint stamp from your post office.

Design your very own elephant stamp, in full color. Telephone the post office to discover if any American stamps portray elephants.

(007, Science, Synthesis, Originality)

A BIG WIG

Two men owned a giant panda bear,

Who constantly got into their hair!

Boo Boo Bear was oh so very big,

He just removed one very large wig,

And threw it way, way over there!

Now if the wig held 30,242 strands of hair,

And each strand weighed .001 of an ounce,

How much weight of the wig was really there,

Onto which the panda bear did pounce?

(007, Mathematics, Problem Solving, Multiplication, Decimals)

GA141

CULTURE CLUB

Many different ethnic groups display their own forms of clothing, food, modes of transportation, language, chants and/or music, and products for which they are famous. For example, in one Indian culture, birthdays are celebrated in teepees by sometimes creating eagles out of grass, playing tribal music, and seeing that a very special time is had by all, from the tribal elders on down to the little children.

Invent your own unique culture by making a list under each of the categories given above and stating exactly what the various topics represent in your culture. Draw a picture of your "typical family."

(007, Social Studies, Synthesis)

A YELLOW FELLOWSHIP

Yellow is the color of gold, butter, ripe lemons, bananas, grapefruit, egg yolks, as well as being a color lying between orange and green on the color spectrum. The color yellow also implies a person who is cowardly or a newspaper which prints cheap and sensational articles, known as yellow journalism.

Create a yellow collage and write a limerick about it.

Or use all five of your senses and write how yellow feels, sounds, tastes, smells, and looks.

Or design a yellow scrapbook, using magazine pictures, real-life objects, and your own works of art. Write yellow descriptions for each page and use as many similes as possible.

Decide whether or not yellow would be an acceptable color for your bedroom. Give reasons.

(007, English, Synthesis, Evaluation)

BART'S HEART WAS STOLEN

In a class that taught simple art,
There attended a creative boy named Bart.
Bart liked to use the rolling paint cart,
Or at least used a very big part.
One day someone stole Bart's heart,
You could even see ole Cupid's dart!
As an offering of love Bart gave Kart a tart,
Which he found down the street at the Mini-Mart.
Now the answer we want from you today,
Is to figure out that if the tart had 321 calories, what's that you say?
She ate two thirds of the tart, 'cause that's just her way?
How many thirds of the tart were left, olé,
And how many calories were contained in what was eaten this day?

(007, Mathematics, Problem Solving, Fractions, Division)

A RACCOON'S TYPE OF COOPERATION

Raccoons are very intelligent creatures who are very wise about cooperation. They frequently work together to forge for water and food. In addition, they may help each other reach places that wouldn't be accessible to just one.

Why is cooperation such an important skill to have? In regard to working in a group successfuly, list ten rules for "perfect" cooperation.

(007, Science, Comprehension, Fluency)

A NIGHT ON THE TOWN

Steve vacuumed the rug and dusted the place,

And then he found out he had dirt on his face.

He decided to go out and enjoy life for awhile,

So he put on his $120.00 jacket and went out in style.

His $42.50 shoes and $83.00 alligator belt,

And his emblem of $19.49 made out of felt...

Went perfectly, delightfully with his $425.00 suit,

As well as his $98.79 brown leather boot(s).

Now the question of the hour for you to find out,

Is the total price of Steve's outfit so neat and so stout!

(007, Math, Problem Solving, Addition, Money)

MYTHICAL CREATURES

The gods and goddesses of mythology appear in many forms. The ancient Greeks, Hindus, and Egyptians all believe that at least one or more of their gods or goddesses had either human shapes, heads of animals, or other unusual characteristics.

Develop your own mythological creatures and create a myth, using special powers and whatever else you can think up.

(007, English, Synthesis)

GA1415

INSIGHTFUL CYCLES

There are currently unicycles (one-wheel), bicycles (two-wheels), and tricycles (three-wheels). All of these have different riding purposes. Tricycles are usually ridden by tots or seniors, bicycles can be ridden by folks of all ages, and unicycles are usually ridden in circuses or shows. There are also other different kinds of cycles like racing cycles and motorcycles.

Design a new kind of bicycle with five wheels and two seats, and call it a pentacycle.

(008, Science, Synthesis)

A THREE-TOED FOOT

The zebra's ancient relatives displayed no more than three toes on each foot, which compares equally to all the ancestors of the horse family. Modern day zebras display one toe on each foot, which is also encased in a hard hoof.

"Horses and zebras run on their fingernails." Try and discover what this statement means and then write a short poem about it.

(008, Science, Analysis, Synthesis)

GA14

YOU HAVE WON THE LOTTERY!

You have just won a lottery of $2,000,000.00. However, you are such a generous person that you have decided to give away $100.00 to a different worthy soul every hour on the hour. How many total hours would it take to spend all your money? How many days? How many weeks? And how would you decide who you would give the money to?

(008, Mathematics, Problem Solving, Evaluation, Multiplication, Time)

ON TOP OF THE WORLD

You're literally "on top of the world,"

Now how do you get down?

You have many options before you,

"But which one is best?" you frown.

Make a list of twenty ways,

That you can leave the top...

And when you reach the twentieth,

If you have more time, don't stop!

One way might be to parachute,

Another might be to ski.

Now it's your turn to brainstorm ways,

On which to make your flee!

(008, English, Fluency)

93

SYNTHESIZING SONGS

The Beatles sang in "I Am the Walrus," "I am he as you are he and you are me and we are all together."

In "Long May You Run" by the Stephen-Stills-Neil Young Band, the title song says:
"We've been through some things together,
With trunks of memories still to come.
We found things to do in stormy weather,
Long may you run.
Long may you run..."

Bill Quateman is quoted as singing:
"Everyone I knew
Used to dance
Without any shoes but
The times have changed and
Only the bears are the same."

In Cat Steven's album by the same name, Cat sings:
"Now I've been happy lately,
Thinking about the good things to come.
And I believe it could be, something good has begun.
Oh I've been smiling lately,
Dreaming about the world as one
And I believe it could be,
That someday it's going to come."

A synthesis of these four songs might look something like this:
I am he as you are he and you are me and we are all together,
We found things to do in stormy weather.
Everyone I knew used to dance but now the times have changed
I've been happy lately
Dreaming about the world as one
I've got trunks of memories still to come
Long may I run.
I believe that someday it's going to come
Long may we run.

Your job is to collect four favorite lyrics of your own, find a link between them, synthesize the lyrics, and create a brand-new song. If you are really ambitious, put your original song to music. Good luck!

(008, English, Synthesis)

GA14

DO YOU HAVE A SWEET TOOTH?

Everyone has a sweet tooth and what better way to cure it than with candy? Candy comes smooth, chewy, mouth watering, hard, soft, mellow, and yellow.

Write ten candy captions or slogans for pictures of candy you find in a magazine. Or design a magazine ad for "Freebees," a new nutty, crunchy, marshmallowy, chocolate surprise.

(008, English, Synthesis)

A DRAGON THAT DOESN'T BREATHE FIRE

Komodo dragons are the largest of all lizards. They can be nine feet (2.7 m) long and weigh more than 200 pounds (90 kg). A Komodo dragon starred in a movie with Matthew Broderick called *The Freshman*.

Research the Komodo dragons and find out all you can about them. Create an informative poem, using all the facts you discovered.

(008, Science, Comprehension, Synthesis)

GA1415

YUKON JACK

In the olden days, way, way, WAY BACK,
There lived a guy named Finnius Yukon Jack,
Old Jack really had a great ole knack,
For filling up more than one brown paper sack.
He filled the sacks with many a tack.
And then stopped in for a lighthearted snack!
The stack of paper bags filled a small shack,
Until there were 1023 bags waiting for the pack.
Yukon Jack was pretty much of a yack,
And liked to dress up all in black.
He never received very much flack,
And he loved his secretary and gave her a big SMACK!
My question for you if you've got the knack,
Is to figure out how much these bundles of sacks with tacks.
Cost to those who are waiting for their packs,
If 14 bags each costing $10.50 per bundle fit each stack,
And if you can solve this, you deserve a plaque!

(008, Mathematics, Problem Solving, Multiplication)

FAMOUS NAMOUS

Imagine that your class is involved in researching famous people. You have gotten involved with one of these famous individuals and have learned quite a bit about his life.

Pretend you are an historically important individual, dress in appropriate costume, and present to your class a serious or humorous "autobiographical poem."

(008, Social Studies, Analysis)

GA14

SNACK CITY

There are lots of different kinds of snack foods like popcorn, cookies, candy, peanuts, chips, pies, cakes, and ice cream.

Your job is to create a very new kind of snack which will salivate not only pre-teens and teenagers but adults as well. Prepare an ad for the radio which will share your idea with the world.

(008, English, Synthesis)

LIVING IN A BUBBLE

Did you realize that the air you are breathing today is the same air that the dinosaurs breathed millions of years ago? (Give or take some pollution!)

Imagine having a disease that forced you to live in a "bubble" all your life because you were allergic to outside air and the germs it contained. Write a paper about your experiences while comparing your life with that of a normal child.

(008, Science, Synthesis, Analysis)

ABOMINABLE SNOWMAN

Sasquatch or the Abominable Snowman as some refer to it has been "tracked" with footprints up to 14" (35.56 cm) in length and that's where the name Big Foot came from. These creatures have been reported to have been seen in forests for hundreds of years. Some believe that since both Sasquatch and Big Foot originated somewhere in Asia, they may have been cousins.

If each adult Big Foot moved with 6-foot (1.8 m) strides, how many footprints would be found within 1 mile (1.61 km)? How about in 5 miles (8.05 km)? What if a group of 10 adult Big Foots moved 2.5 miles (4 km) in one day, how many footprints would they leave? If young Big Foots moved with 3-foot (4.83 km) strides, how many footprints would they leave in a mile (kilometer). Finally, if a tribe of 13 adult Big Foots and 7 young Big Foots traveled 6 miles (9.66 km), exactly how many footprints would be made?

(008, Mathematics, Problem Solving, Multiplication)

INTERIOR DECORATING

As building progressed through the centuries, from tents to skyscrapers, different services have been required for the interiors. Contact an interior decorator and ask him/her to come and talk with your class. Prepare a ten-question interview, including questions about the history of interior decorating, how it has changed through the years, specific job qualifications for an interior decorator, description, etc.

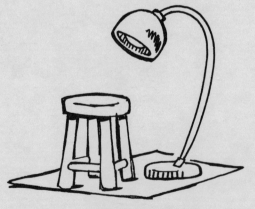

(008, Social Studies, Analysis)

MOVE INTO THE GROOVE

Many people believe that only living things can move or run. However, they are very wrong.

Name at least twenty nonliving things that can move or run, and then at least three nonliving things that can make copies of themselves.

For example: A drill can run!

(008, Science, Fluency)

WORLDWIDE PEACE

Suppose worldwide peace was declared at midnight but no one else knew this fact. Your mission was to tell four people every hour on the hour until ten o'clock in the morning. At the same time, each of the four people each hour would tell four of their friends every hour on the hour. Then each of their friends would tell four more people every hour on the hour, etc.

How many total people would have been contacted by 10:00 a.m.?

(008, Mathematics, Problem Solving, Multiplication)

GA1415

UNUSUAL SNAKES

The smallest snakes are thread snakes which measure only 1 to 1.3 cm long and are so thin they could glide through the hole left in a normal pencil if the lead was removed. The longest snake ever kept in captivity was a 9-meter reticulated python. In the wild there are reports of some snakes like the anacondas that measure up to 42 meters long.

Write a short story which couples the smallest and the largest snakes in a unique adventure tale.

(008, Science, Synthesis)

MANY MEMBERS OF MEDICINE

Many members of medium-sized medicine-making men made much medicine over millions of years, so much so that a multitude of 65 mermaids each moved 329 crates of medicine to a messenger during a meteor shower 14 miles (22.54 km) up the messy mainland.

How many total crates were moved very meticulously, and if each mermaid moved crates 14 miles (22.54 km), how many total miles (kilometers) were moved across?

(008, Mathematics, Problem Solving, Multiplication)

GA1415

THE SUPERMARKET OF THE FUTURE

The modern design of most supermarkets involves long rows or aisles containing different groups of foods, in addition to produce areas and refrigerators for cold products. No matter which type of grocery store you enter, the layout is pretty much the same.

Your job is to design the supermarket of the future. Obtain a large piece of graph paper and make it to scale. How will you determine how much an item will cost? How will the total bill be figured? How will you determine where the sale items will be?

(008, Social Studies, Synthesis)

GRAVE SAYINGS

An epitaph is either a poem or statement about a person which is imprinted upon his/her gravestone after he/she is gone.

For example:

> Here lies the body of Steve S. Still
>
> Who died and is buried under a windowsill
>
> Steve lived his life in the best of ways
>
> And chose here to live out all of his days.

Your job is to choose two famous individuals who have already passed on and two famous persons who are still alive and write "make-believe" epitaphs for each of the four of them.

(008, English, Synthesis)

GA1415

A SLUG CAN BE SLUGGISH

The Spanish dancer is a glamorous name for one type of nocturnal sea slug. This slug is an invertebrate and uses its flexible abdomen to grab onto any surface. It swims by wiggling through the water.

The word *slug* has many different meanings. Without using the dictionary to begin with, write down all the meanings which you already know. Now, in both an encyclopedia and a dictionary, look up the term *slug* and make a list of all the different definitions which you didn't know already. Develop and design a perfect slug habitat. (Figure out which definition this slug refers to!) Finally, brainstorm all the different kinds of slugs there could possibly be, both real and imaginary.

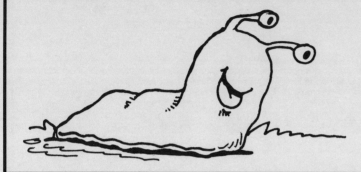

(008, Science, Fluency, Synthesis)

THE BANK THAT SANK!

A big BANK sat in the middle of town,
They say it SANK way under and way down,
Fat old HANK stood on the first step,
One fowl PRANK left HANK minus pep.
HANK took a CRANK and tried to lift the BANK,
But HANK went BLANK and the BANK RESANK.
A little THANK you was not coming soon.
For all FRANK cared, HANK could go to the moon!
A redwood PLANK was placed right under the BANK,
And a SPANK was given to a little boy named TANK,
The smell was RANK from under the ground,
And it STANK so bad not a flower could be found.
The redwood PLANK SHRANK and was of no use,
And the BANK was left sitting under much abuse.
Now, if 15 ten-foot PLANKS were shoved under the BANK,
And each one SHRANK at 2" per day, and that's FRANK.
If the BANK was underground for thirteen whole days,
How much was left of the PLANKS in the town of Bankerways?

(008, Mathematics, Problem Solving)

AN IMPORTANT MISSION

Every day in the U.S., companies are going under (falling apart) because of poor management, union pressures, business takeovers, or lack of funds. When a big business falls apart, many people lose their jobs and the company can no longer service others.

Imagine that you are a business owner who runs a company that does a very important service—you help the elderly to receive meals once a day, and these are people who might otherwise not eat. You have little money left to provide services and the city wants to close you down.

What plan of action(s) would you take to make sure your business stays open?

(008, Social Studies, Analysis)

BLUE, I'M SO BLUE...

I've heard of the famous Blue Devils,
A bright bluebell and a funky blueberry.
I've seen Bluebeard and Blue Bird,
And been on the Blue Grass Ferry.
One of my friends is a blue jacket in the Navy and works nights,
The blue gum tree in my backyard has grown to new heights.
I caught a bluegill while worrying about Blue Chip Stocks yesterday,
Saw a blue fox and a blue crab underneath some blocks that got in my way.
I blue penciled out my first copy.
While a blue whale read my book,
I ordered the blue plate special,
While a blue-blooded Englishman took a look,
A bluebonnet was found on a bluish jacket, no lie,
And a blue flag iris really caught my eye!
Finish this story starter, "I can't do homework! I'm so blue!"
Or design a blue flag for a blue country and an anthem, oh so true.
Or list five synonyms for the word *blue* and the haiku about the sky,
Or write a story about your stay in Blueland that's got you wondering why.

(008, English, Synthesis)

103

HIPPO NOT A TRUE HORSE

Hippopotamus is a Greek word meaning "river horse." Of course, hippos aren't really horses. But they can live nearly as long as a horse—forty-nine years.

Research the horse and the hippo. Make a list of ten facts about each animal. Then compare and contrast the two animals and make statements as to their similarities and differences.

(008, Science, Analysis)

PIRANHAS ARE ONE VICIOUS FISH!

In the waters of the Amazon lives a very unique type of fish called a piranha. Approximately one school of piranhas can devour a 100-pound (45 kg) animal in one minute after they have smelled the scent of blood. Being no more than 14" (35.56 cm) long, having razor sharp teeth, maintaining powerful jaws and residing in large schools, piranhas are a possible threat to man as well as other large animals and large fish.

If 800 piranhas ate a 100-pound (45 kg) animal in one minute, how many ounces (grams) did each piranha eat? Draw a picture of what you think a piranha looks like; then compare your picture with one found in an encyclopedia.

(008, Mathematics, Problem Solving)

GA141

CHINESE COULD TRAVEL FROM THE EARTH TO THE MOON!

Did you know there are more women than men in the U.S.S.R.? For every one hundred women, there are only eighty-five men. Did you know if the total number of people in China stood on each other's shoulders, they could make three chains stretching from the earth to the moon? Did you know about a sixth of the world's oil is not used for fuel but rather for six other items? See if you can discover what they are as well as who the oil producers are, from biggest to smallest.

(008, Social Studies, Anaylsis)

1989-90 WERE INCREDIBLE YEARS!

Quite a few amazing things happened during the years 1989 and 1990. Chinese college students had a major uprising, the East Germans brought down the Berlin Wall, the Iraq takeover of Kuwait, and back at home baseball legend Pete Rose was banned for life from baseball, just to name a few.

Your task is to research one of 1989-90's greatest moments and write an eight-to-sixteen-line poem about the events which occurred. Use as many different resources (encyclopedias, magazines, microfilm, etc.) as you need.

(008, Social Studies, Analysis)

GA1415

COOL LAND, U.S.A.

Travel companies create brochures with photographs or pictures and descriptions of the places they'd like others to visit on their vacations.

Design a travel brochure, taking the reader on a tour of "Cool Land, U.S.A."

(008, Social Studies, Syntheis)

OUT OF LUCK

The word *out* can take on numerous meanings, such as "out of luck," "out of bounds," and "outside." You can be "out of sorts," "out of shape," and "out of money."

Make a list of all the different ways *out* can be used, and then incorporate them into a tall tale.

(008, English, Synthesis)

GA1415

SPORTS GRAFFITI

Graffiti is defined as "drawings or writings on rocks or walls." Graffiti can be found just about anywhere you look: buses, viaducts, sides of buildings, storefronts, and it is usually done on a dare, by lovers in love, or by gangs.

Design a graffiti poster, using only terms, emblems and sayings having to do with sports.

(008, English, Application)

DON'T GUM UP YOUR LIFE!

Chewing gum can gum up a person's teeth as well as affect his sugar intake. However, chewing gum is one of the best-selling products we have in the U.S. today. That means, millions of Americans are chewing it constantly!

Analyze all the different kinds of chewing gum for their individual calorie counts and then create a dieter's notebook.

(008, Science, Analysis)

GA1415

FRIENDS ATTEND THE STOCK CAR RACES!

Stevie, Sally, Stan and Susan all attended the stock car races and ate popcorn, pasta, pickles and peanuts. Each ate a different food and came in a different car: a Camaro, Corvair, Corvette or a Cadillac. Each drove in from either Brownsville, Barkley, Barrymore or Benson.

Now what you need to figure out, using the following clues, is who lives where, drives what and enjoys which food.

The chart below may help you to find the answers. Make an O every time you discover that something is definitely not possible. Put an X every time you discover that something is definitely true. Good luck!

1. Stevie is allergic to salt and nuts.

2. Susan loves big, expensive, luxurious cars.

3. Sally lives in the town with the most letters.

4. Stan loves pickles but hates Camaros.

5. Stevie and Sally have been on rides in her new Corvette.

6. Stan makes his own stock cars in Barrymore.

7. Sally craves peanuts when she's excited.

8. Stevie lives in the city with six letters.

	Popcorn	Pasta	Pickles	Peanuts	Camaro	Corvair	Corvette	Cadillac	Brownsville	Barkley	Barrymore	Benson
Stevie												
Susan												
Sally												
Stan												

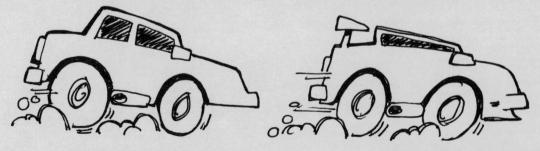

(008, Problem Solving, Logic)

GA14

SHREDDING

A new fad is beginning to catch on in the 90's–snowboarding or shredding. This brand-new fad involves hitting the slopes with a snowboard–a combination of a skateboard and a surfboard. These fiberglass boards can cruise down a slope as fast as 60 mph. Experts say it takes about three days to learn "shredding," and although it's permitted at 75 percent of all ski areas, there is some concern about safety.

Make a list of at least ten safety rules you might instigate as the owner of a ski resort.

(008, Science, Application)

YOU'VE LEARNED 75,000 THINGS A YEAR!

You really ought to take a stand,
And lend an open helping hand.
You might even think to join a band,
And perform a concert at a grandstand!
You might roam clear across the land,
In search of the whitest sand,
Or invent a new kind of cereal brand,
And make sure that it isn't bland.
Now while you're spending all this time,
Just solve one problem and it's no crime.
You've spent ten to thirteen years just finding yourself,
Every year you've tried to jump onto the shelf.
You've learned 75,000 things a year,
And if you remembered them all you'd be without fear.
How many total things have been taught to you,
Since you were born that someday you'll remember too?

(008, Mathematics, Problem Solving, Multiplication)

109

GA1415

MYTHOLOGICAL MONSTER

Greek myths have been around for a long time and have thrilled their readers for many, many years. Some Greek mythological monsters and creatures include Argus, a hundred-eyed giant; Griffin, half-lion and half-eagle; and Hydra, a nine-headed serpent growing two heads for each one that was cut off. The Greeks really had a wild imagination!

Create your very own Greek myth using the creatures listed above as the main characters. Make the myth two to four pages in length and add as many details as possible. Illustrate your myth upon completion.

(008, English, Synthesis, Elaboration)

CITIES OVERTAKE LAND

As we begin to build more and more cities and overtake the land, the poor animals that have been residing there will have no place to live and eventually will die. Their habitats will be destroyed.

How can we, as a society, stop this from occurring? Write an action plan, citing all of your ideas.

(008, Science, Synthesis, Originality)

GA14

MATH DAZZLE

Here's a real math quizzer for you! What is one fourth times one fourth divided by one fourth? How about one half times one half divided by one half? What conclusions can you draw from these two equations?

(008, Mathematics, Analysis)

PERMANENT PICTURES

Have you ever seen a man or woman with a tattoo on some part of his or her body? Well, a tattoo is an unremovable "mark or figure fixed upon the body by the insertion of pigment or paint under the skin or by the production of scars."

Design a picture on paper of what might be an 8" x 11" (20.32 x 27.94 cm) sized tattoo. Make it as detailed as possible.

(008, Social Studies, Elaboration)

GA1415

TELEVISED OR NOT?

If a person is convicted of a brutal crime and is sentenced to death, do you feel his/her execution should be televised to millions of people? Why or why not? Explain your answer in story format, citing lots of reasons for or against.

(008, Social Studies, Evaluation, Elaboration)

NETS WITH PETS

A long time ago aboard a winged jet,

It was destiny for Ralph and Benny to have met.

For below the plane was a big net,

Into which flew many a pet.

Along for a ride was a good vet,

Who was out to settle a terrific bet.

There was something that Benny had started to regret,

And pretty soon he'd just fret and fret.

Well, what we need to discover just from you,

Is if the plane went 13,642 miles from Kalamazoo...

And four new pets were caught at each mile,

While each of the chirping pets had eight babies, birdie style,

How many total birds were caught in the net

On a plane during an outing one doesn't soon forget?

(008, Mathematics, Problem Solving, Multiplication)

GA141

FILLAMENA FLAMINGO

Write a tall tale about Fillamena Flamingo and her brood of fifty fancy but fitful and fierce five-year-old flamingos. Fillamena wasn't fat but rather flimsy, and her five-year-old flamingos were frail and frumpy, if you can imagine that!

Write your tall tale in the biggest exaggerations you can think of!

(008, English, Synthesis)

JOLLY GIRAFFES

Giraffes make quite a majestic sight as they romp and relax in the sun. Giraffes are also one of the tallest creatures ever to have lived. Sometimes giraffes wander a great deal in seach of food. They may spend only a few minutes at one tree before going on to the next to find a few more leaves. The neck of a giraffe is long enough to reach high places, like going into the trees, but it is not long enough to bend down to the ground. When a giraffe wants to drink, it is forced to spread its front legs wide apart or bend its knees.

Paint a watercolor picture of a large group of giraffes at a watering hole.

(008, Science, Synthesis)

GA1415

ANIMAL TALK

Animals are wonderful because we can imagine all kinds of things about them, such as they can fly or talk.

Create an imaginary animal that can do one of the things you like to do (sing, dance, ski, etc.). Design a flip book that shows your animal in action!

(008, Science, Synthesis)

THE GOOD SNAKES

Did you know that many India Indians have far more respect for snakes than for those who tend to charm them? The cobra is deemed "The Good Snake" simply because it eats rats. Indians don't have high feelings for snake charmers because many of them defang their cobras before using them in their acts. That seems a little dishonest, don't you think?

Create a bulletin board display showing off the cobra and demonstrating fifteen interesting facts about this snake.

(008, Science, Knowledge, Originality)

GA1

Answer Key

Sweets for the Sweet, Page 3: 170 food items
Pandamonium, Page 4: 3 elephants
It's All Rock and Roll to Me! Page 5: 71 albums
Flightess Birds, Page 6: any reasonable answer
Eye Spy, Page 9: 47 eyes
This Rattle Doesn't Come from a Baby! Page 10: 600 feet (182.4 m)
Dogs and Their Walks, Page 11: 50 trees
Circus Fever, Page 13: 76 circus performers
The Fishing Flu, Page 14: 174 animals
Modge Podge, Page 15: 209 things seen
A Plant's Defense System, Page 18: 600 ways

Professional Wrestling, Page 22: 2009 lbs., Stevie the King
The Balloon Festival, Page 25: 1036 miles
Two Humps for Camels! Page 27: 5000 shipped each year
Newspaper Antics, Page 27: 333 things
Skaters Galore, Page 28: 415 skaters
Marsupial Mamas, Page 30: 140 babies
Dancing and Prancing, Page 31: 720 minutes
Gramp's Rampage, Page 33: $11.00 per umbrella
No Lie'n, Page 34: 1059, 486, 1434, 1026, 870, 552
Five, Six, Pick Up Sticks, Page 35: 444 items

The Dude Ranch, Page 37: 9.33 bananas
Happy Hero, Page 38: 528 lbs.
Splurging While Shopping, Page 39: $245.22
Take Pride in Prides, Page 40: 520 lions
Sport Nuts! Page 41, 293 sports players
Many Movie Moms, Page 42: $330.00
Skater Dudes, Page 43: 164 minutes
Basketball Fever, Page 44: 36 baskets
Modern Day Robin Hood, Page 45: $15,050
Who's the Best? Page 50: 1020 total questions
Super Strikes, Page 51: 1056 strides

Potpourri of Mathematics, Page 55: 32, 55, 4, 57, 78, 1452, 42, 74

Adding Numbers, Page 56: 210 total

An Elephant Stampede, Page 57: $40,000

Razzmatazz! Page 59: $3.11

Air-Bound? Page 61: 36 seconds

She Has Paid Her Due, Page 63: $13.50

WIllie's Night Out, Page 65: 5:42 went for gas, returned at 5:59

Frogs and Felines Fight! Page 66: 9680 feathers

Rand, the Donkey, Page 68: 315 minutes

Penguins Find Gold, Page 71: 15% of the gold

A Dinosaur Does Good, Page 73: $20 for rides, $58.50 for toys–total $78.50

A Racing Riot, Page 74: 10 lbs. of flour were left

It's a Party! Page 75: 195 attended

Bought and Sold! Page 76: $50 was made

Excellent Exponents, Page 78: 10^9 = billion, 10^{12} = trillion, 10^{15} = quadrillion, 10^{18} = quintillion, 10^{21} = sextillion, 10^{24} = septillion, 10^{27} = octillion, 10^{33} = decillion, 10^{42} = tredecillion, 10^{54} = septendecillion, 10^{60} = novemdecillion, 10^{100} = googol

Listen to the Heartbeat, Page 82: 4320 per hour, 72 per minute

Ash Revisited, Page 83: $2497.51

Consecutive Numbers, Page 86: any acceptable pairs

A Big Wig, Page 88: 30.242 ounces

Bart's Heart Was Stolen, Page 90: $1/3$ left, 214 calories

A Night on the Town, Page 91: $788. 78

You Have Won the Lottery, Page 93: 20,000 hours, 833 days, 119 weeks

Yukon Jack, Page 96: $147

Abominable Snowman, Page 98: 880; 4400; 22,000; 1760; 142,560

Worldwide Peace, Page 99: over one million

Many Members of Medicine, Page 100: 21,385 crates; 910 miles (1465.10 km)

The Bank That Sank! Page 102: 7 feet, 10 inches (21.28 m, 25.4 cm)

Piranhas Are One Vicious Fish! Page 104: 2 ounces (56.7 kg) each

Friends Attend the Stock Car Races, Page 108: Stevie–popcorn, Camaro, Benson; Susan–pasta, Cadillac, Brownsville; Sally–peanuts, Corvette, Barkley; Stan–pickles, Corvair, Barrymore

Math Dazzle, Page 111: $1/4$ and $1/2$

Nets with Pets, Page 112: 436,544 birds

GA141

Bibliography

Windows to the World by Nancy Everix, Good Apple, Inc., 1984.

Mysteries and Marvels of the Reptile World by Ian Spellerberg and Marit McKerchar, EDC Publishing, 1984.

The Instant Answer Book of Countries by Annabel Warrender and Jerry Tyler, Usborne Publishing LTD, 1978.

If You're Trying to Teach Kids to Write, You've Gotta Have This Book! by Marjorie Frank, Incentive Publications, 1979.

Once upon a Question by Warren Siegmond, 1975.

The World Almanac and Book of Facts, 1989.

Guinness Book of World Records, 1989.

More Fascinating Facts by Davis Louis, 1979.

Photo Fun by David Webster, 1973.

In the Air by Graham Weston, 1983.

Famous Planes by Brenda Thompson and Rosemary Giesen, 1977.

Calliope by Greta Barclay Lipson, Ed.D., and Jane Romatowski, Ed.D., Good Apple, Inc., 1981.

Let Loose on Mother Goose by Terry Graham, Incentive Publications, 1982.

The Science and Sound of Spelling by Dr. Anna Marie Gruber and Gladys L. Jackson, 1971.

Aircraft at Work by Mary Elting, 1964.

Math for Smarty Pants by Marilyn Burns, Little, Brown, and Company, 1982.

Science World, February 9, 1990, Vol 46, No. 11.

Zoobooks, Quality Productions, Inc., San Diego, California.

    Elephants by John, B. Wexo, 1980 and 1986.

    Animal Wonders by John B. Wexo, August 1988.

    Bears by John B. Wexo, 1982.

    Snakes by John B. Wexo, July 1987.

    Camels by John B. Wexo, November 1986.

    Wild Horses by John B. Wexo, February 1987.

    Endangered Animals by John B. Wexo, May 1987.

    Little Cats by John B. Wexo, October 1988.

Night Animals by John B. Wexo, February 1987.

Wolves by John B. Wexo, July 1986.

Insects I by John B. Wexo, May 1989.

The Apes by John B. Wexo, 1981.

Gorillas by John B. Wexo, 1984.

Baby Animals by John B. Wexo, November 1986.

Prehistoric Zoobooks by John B. Wexo, 1989.

Giraffes by John B. Wexo, 1987.

Lions by John B. Wexo, June 1989.

Baby Animals II by John B. Wexo, November 1989.

*Ostriches, Emus...*by John B. Wexo, January 1990.

Rattlesnakes by John B. Wexo, August 1989.

Polar Bears by Timothy Levi Biel, 1985.

City Animals by Timothy Levi Biel, 1984.

Skunks by Timothy Levi Biel, 1988.

GA1415